COSMO'S
RED-HOT
SEX
SECRETS

Tons of Naughty, Pleasure-Maxing Moves that Will Send You Both Over the Edge

The Editors of COSMOPOLITAN

COSMO'S
RED-HOT
SEX
SECRETS

Tons of Naughty, Pleasure-Maxing Moves that Will Send You Both Over the Edge

The Editors of COSMOPOLITAN

HEARST BOOKS
A division of Sterling Publishing Co., Inc.

New York / London
www.sterlingpublishing.com

Contents

Discover a secret hot zone all men have.

33
Sex up your bedroom!

CONTENTS

182
Intensify your bedroom bond.

the main event   120

163
The magic ingredient to mind-blowing sex

Preface

Millions of voracious Cosmo readers rely on the candid and superfun way the magazine gives sex advice. In fact, many of you have been begging us to put all of our infinite sexual know-how together in one place so you can have a complete guide to mind-blowing sex at your fingertips.

Well, your wait is over. You have in your hands *Cosmo's Guide to Red-Hot Sex*. There are some books that are meant for your coffee table, but this one belongs on your *bedside* table—since you'll want to keep all the detailed instructional info we've compiled here within easy reach. Care for a tease?

From the very first page, you'll realize that this book aims to elevate your sexual status to goddess level. That means introducing you to the idea that great sex starts before there's even another person in the room. Building your arousal through simple but stimulating mental exercises and body moves is one of the keys to amazing sex.

You'll also learn how to make a guy ache for you all day (an endeavor you'll enjoy *almost* as much as he will). Once you do get your hands on him, we'll arm you with an arsenal of smokin'-hot sex tricks. (Warning: These pleasure-producing techniques may render a lover temporarily speechless. You're okay with that, right?) One highlight: We'll take you on a guided tour of a man's M zone—a nerve-dense region that few women know about. The stroke secrets we've perfected work wonders on that area…and on every inch of a man's body.

As you know, Cosmo is famous for creating some of the most innovative sexual techniques around. Ever heard of our celebrated hair-scrunchie and glazed-donut tricks? They're in here. And you're going to find out how to perform them masterfully. All this info is punctuated by testimonials from blissed-out guys who recount their most memorable experiences…in juicy detail.

Besides being packed with suggestions that will make a guy's toes curl, this bedroom bible will help you find your own orgasm triggers and then teach you how to get him to hit them perfectly. And for women who have difficulty climaxing, we pinpoint the main factor that will take you over the edge. Plus: You'll discover 21 sizzling sex positions to try starting—why not?—tonight!

Of course, since truly satisfying sex requires experimentation, it's inevitable that some awkward—and yes, embarrassing—moments will crop up from time to time. Not to worry. We have solutions for conquering even your toughest carnal challenges. Lastly, we'll tell you how to make the most of those after-sex moments, including how to cement the bond you have with your man.

So if you're ready to boost your sexual gratification to unimaginable heights, go ahead…turn the page…. ■

The Editors of
COSMOPOLITAN

A lot of women don't start thinking about sex until they hit the bedroom and begin stripping off their clothes. And that's a huge mistake—one that cuts their pleasure potential way short. A key ingredient to a really amazing sexual experience is getting in the mood long before an erotic encounter. In fact, experts such as Laura Berman, PhD, author of *The Passion Prescription,* say that thinking about sex before you actually have it is a supereffective way to fuel arousal. And the more aroused you are in the hours before having sex, the more responsive your body is likely to be once you get down to it.

Women aren't the only ones who can benefit from a little sexual simmering. Men are also more likely to have a hot romp if they've been looking forward to it all day…with a little help from you, of course. Since 85 percent of 20- to 30-year-old males think about sex every couple of hours, why not exploit your man's innately naughty mind-set? You may think you have zero control over the X-rated images that course through his brain, but the truth is, there are all sorts of surprising ways you can stoke his desire for you.

So let's get this party started!

ay preplay preplay preplay preplay preplay prep

A sexy self-fulfilling prophecy: Thinking about an incredible night of sex makes it more likely to happen.

Getting in the Mood

▶ Setting the stage for some seriously great sex doesn't just happen with a perfectly planned sequence of events—a bottle of wine, candles, and seductive music. (Okay, those things do help....) But the fact is, you have the power to put yourself on the path to an amazing night long before you even see the guy.

This might be an entirely new concept—scratch that—this *will* be a new concept to you, but it's true: The secret to phenomenal sex doesn't begin when you're in the same room with your lover...it starts when you're all by yourself.

REVEL IN YOUR NAKEDNESS

If you give yourself license to enjoy your sensuality all day, you'll discover something pretty exciting: that you feel hotter than ever for a fab romp later on. With that in mind, here are a few ideas for getting in touch with the sexiness of your own skin:

■ Indulge in a set of supersoft, high-thread-count sheets and slip into bed nude...even if you're alone.

■ Postshower, slather on body oil and take a moment to enjoy the feeling of your curves.

■ In the a.m., try a sex-kitten pose (in the buff) to send a flood of erogenous energy coursing through your bod. Start on your hands and knees with your back relaxed and in a neutral position. As you inhale, arch your back fully and tilt your pelvis forward while

Smoothing on a faux glow can boost your body confidence.

INSTASEXY TRICKS

...Apply self-tanner with a subtle shimmer quality.

...Wear drop-dead sexy lingerie under your work clothes.

...Get a tall, narrow mirror that tilts up slightly.

...Keep a hot picture of yourself in plain sight in your pad.

lifting your tailbone. As you exhale, curl your pelvis under so your back is rounded, like a cat stretching. Think about drawing your breath down the center of your torso and engulfing your body with sexual heat, says Jacquie Noelle Greaux, coauthor of *Better Sex Through Yoga*.

■ When choosing what to wear in the morning, pick fabrics that glide across your skin: silk, cashmere, and satin will all make you feel soft and sexy. Likewise, lightly mist your bra and undies (except the crotch) with your favorite fragrance to heighten your awareness of your sultry self. Jasmine, rose, bergamot, and sandalwood are ingredients that can get you in passion mode, according to Rochelle Bloom, president of the Fragrance Foundation.

BREAK A SWEAT

Another way to ramp up your libido (and make your body even more beautiful) is to break a sweat. A mini biology lesson: During exercise, the body produces endorphins, which create feelings of exhilaration, happiness, and calmness. Increased blood flow throughout the body (including the pelvis) increases sexual arousal. Plus, extra amounts of the hormone adrenaline, which is released during exercise, can

She's wearing perfume in some *very* unexpected places.

also lead to elevated levels of sexual arousal. When you think about it, working out for the sake of priming yourself for sex is just as good a reason—if not a better one—as it is for shrinking your waist, don't you think?

ENTER FANTASYLAND

There's one more good reason to head to the gym: You're bound to see some hard-bodied guys there who can inspire a new sex fantasy…or two. But we're sure you don't always need to see guys in the flesh to conjure up a thrilling vision—maybe it takes the simple idea of getting a sponge bath from a hot stranger or something more explicit, like playing naughty games with an entire soccer team, to work you up.

Whatever it is, exploring a sexy scene (during a.m. shower

Feel Sexier Naked

When you're in the nude, it can be hard not to be distracted by a body hang-up or two—whether you're fretting about a few extra pounds, pesky cellulite, A-cup breasts, or any other real or imaginary imperfection. Of course, you know it's silly to obsess about this stuff, but it's a hard habit to break. The real problem though: These insecurities can get in the way of enjoying yourself in the sack. Luckily, learning to love the bod

you have has more to do with your mental attitude than your actual reflection in a mirror. To get an "I'm hot" mind-set:

Talk Up the Good Stuff

This scene will definitely ring a bell: You say "I have no butt" or "Man, I look so fat," and then your friend swears up and down that it's not true. You know why you do it—it feels good to get reassurance. But you don't need a pal to prop you up—you can be your own support system. Here's how: Make a deal with yourself that every time you think something bad about your body ("My thighs are so huge"), you have to wipe it out with a strong positive statement you say to yourself ("My thighs feel so good when they're wrapped around my guy"). For quick inspiration, reflect on how much pleasure your body brings you—when you're exercising, putting lotion on your legs, or having amazing sex. Think of them as mini pep talks you have with yourself.

Work It When You Walk

Can't see how a confident strut will skyrocket your body image and sex appeal? Consider Jennifer Lopez. Her brazenness about showing off her admittedly ample tush—onstage, in videos, on the red carpet—encourages you to buy into the idea that she has the best butt in the world. Practice your own sexy strut until it becomes second nature: "Allow your torso to release up and away from your

hip joints so your legs can move freely beneath you—think up, up, up," says Kate Kobak, certified instructor in New York City in the Alexander Technique, a method for improving balance and flexibility. When you walk, put one foot slightly in front of the other like a runway model does. This causes your hips to sway ever so slightly. And take your sweet time.

If a guy wants to go to bed with you, then rest assured, he already finds you sexy.

Remember: He's Hot for Your Bod

We assume guys are supercritical of our bodies. Wrong! Men may salivate over some girl's perfect belly or breasts on TV, but in real life, they don't dissect our bits and pieces as much as we think they do. In fact, behind closed doors, men admit to being intimidated by women who look like models. So chill out. If a guy wants to go to bed with you, then rest assured, he already finds you sexy.

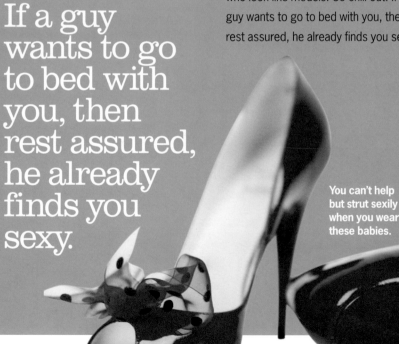

You can't help but strut sexily when you wear these babies.

time or in between appointments at work, for example) can really get your juices flowing by stimulating blood flow to your genitals and putting you in a more sensual, revved-for-sex zone, says Barbara Keesling, PhD, author of *The Good Girl's Guide to Bad Girl Sex*.

As you play out arousing scenes in your head, physical changes happen: your breath quickens, your nipples harden, and you feel a wet heat radiating from between your legs—the result of your vaginal walls contracting, causing a lubricating fluid to be secreted. Forming that mind-body connection is one of the secret ingredients of great-sex prep, because over time, your body becomes conditioned to be more easily stimulated from those racy thoughts. The more stimulated you are, the stronger your craving for sex will be.

HOW TO GENERATE A SEXY STORY LINE

Frisky thoughts beget more frisky thoughts, meaning once you tap into a fantasy that makes your pulse race, naughty scenes will flood your brain. Here, ideas for how to start manufacturing those visions.

Think With Your Panties All Day

Start tracking what excites you. Let's say you're cruising to work when you suddenly find yourself drooling over a hot highway billboard of a guy whose manhood looks as though it's trying to break free of his jeans. Or you spot a sexy couple making out and envision what they'll be doing to each other later that night. Be aware of

images that you find sexy or arousing and let your imagination begin to percolate.

Take a Star Turn

Fantasies are like fingerprints—no two are identical. But there is one universal component: You have to be the focus of the action, whether that puts you at the center of a sizzling threesome or in full view of a sexual encounter being acted out for your eyes only.

"Many women like to watch and be watched," explains Melinda Gallagher, founder of CAKE, an entertainment and educational company that promotes female sexual empowerment. "Start your fantasy scene simply: Think about someone watching you undress and see where that idea leads you."

Peruse Erotica

If you find yourself in short supply of real-world inspiration, try reading an erotic short story or popping in a dirty DVD. "Pornographic films serve as visual validation of things we might only dream of trying," says Gallagher. And sexy movies come in different degrees—from very tame to hard-core skin flicks. "Watch one by yourself to see what stirs you," says Ava Cadell, PhD, author of *The Pocket Idiot's Guide to Oral Sex*.

"Fantasies are about losing your inhibitions, so don't censor your thoughts." Let each scene wash over you, paying attention to what, in particular, pushes your hot buttons. Then put yourself in the flick, casting the guy of your choice as the male lead, says Cadell.

HOW TO REALLY GET IN TOUCH WITH YOUR BOD

Making it a point to think about sex more frequently and to spin titillating fantasies has a clear side effect: It encourages your body to get in on the action. Heed that call by masturbating. Not only does it supply a fantastic release for it's own sake, but it can be an important step in setting the stage for ultrasatisfying sex with a partner. How so? Because before you can hit the big peaks with your guy, it helps to get a handle on the touches that really send you over the edge. Some suggestions for self-play:

■ Draw a bubble bath and begin massaging your inner thighs and running your hands over your tummy and your breasts. Now circle your nipples with your fingertip, then gently tug on them—it may trigger tingles down below. Zero in on your hot spots by getting even more hands-on. "Your fingers are ideal tools for learning what type of pressure, speed, and stroke works the best," says Sadie Allison, DHS, sex educator and author of *Tickle His Pickle*. Let your hands wander south, tracing the sensitive folds of your inner labia. Or try lightly tapping your clitoris—the supersensitive organ (it contains an estimated 8,000 nerve endings) that's tucked inside the top portion of the inner lips of your vulva. Some women find the water flow from a faucet splashing on their clitoris to be an extremely pleasurable sensation.

■ Outside the tub, try placing one or two fingers on your clitoris and stroke in a circular motion. (If that's too intense, stimulate it indirectly by using your whole hand to massage your mons pubis, the mound where your pubic hair grows.)

■ Try some popular stroking styles: Use one or more fingers

"Your fingers are ideal tools for learning what type of stroke and pressure works."

Enhance Your Solo Experience By...

1 Playing slow music or lighting candles to set a sexy mood

2 Emptying your bladder first—it will relax your body

3 Moaning out loud—vocalizing your pleasure can be a turn-on

4 Experimenting with room temperature—some like it hot; others, cold

to glide up, over, and around your clitoral area, tracing the number eight. You'll cover the clitoris and the inner labia. Or hold two fingers out straight, side by side, and run them north to south and east to west over the width and length of your entire pleasure zone. A more advanced method: Use your index and ring fingers to hold open your labia. This frees up your middle finger to stroke the tip of your clitoris. You'll know that your manual maneuvers are working when your genitals feel fuller or hotter as blood circulation increases in that area, ideally setting off orgasmic contractions.

■ For more advanced self-pleasuring: Stimulate your G-spot—a spongy, dime-size area on the front wall of your vagina about 2 to 4 inches in. To locate it, insert your index finger into your vagina and crook it toward your

stomach in a "come here" gesture. If you experience an orgasm, you'll notice that it's deliciously different from a clitoral orgasm, which usually only causes contractions in the first third of the vagina. "A G-spot orgasm triggers spasms throughout the pelvic region," says Los Angeles relationship coach Felice Dunas, PhD.

■ Don't be afraid to experiment. If you want to learn how to orgasm while having doggie-style sex, then get on all fours during your solo trips. Or if you yearn for your vagina to be more orgasmically sensitive like your clitoris, try this maneuver: Use one hand on your clitoris and the other on your vaginal opening to stimulate both simultaneously, occasionally working one hot spot at a time. "By doing this, your body starts to associate one sensation with the other,"

Keep your panties on for a bit to buffer the intense buzz of a vibrator.

says Steve Bodansky, PhD, co-author of *To Bed or Not to Bed*. "Pretty soon, touching one place will trigger a response in the other." Pretty cool, huh?

■ Try using a vibrator—it often provides the strongest and most consistent form of stimulation. Begin by working the vibrator over your clitoris. (You may want to keep your panties on at first as a buffer; the buzz can be intense.) Then tease yourself by alternating speeds as your desire builds. A word of caution: Too much humming can potentially cause your nerve endings to become desensitized temporarily, so don't resort to using a vibrator exclusively. Getting acquainted with these magical sex toys will give you a head start when you get to the "Buzzy Bed Play" chapter of this book. There you'll learn how to incorporate a vibrator into your lovemaking sessions with a man. ■

KEGELS CRASH COURSE

Kegel exercises are the rhythmic clenching and unclenching of the pubococcygeus (PC) muscles, part of the pelvic floor that supports your bladder, uterus, rectum, and vagina. The stronger they are, the deeper and longer orgasms will be.

HERE'S THE OTHER KEGEL ADVANTAGE: Just doing them will turn you on. "A Kegels workout boosts blood flow to your clitoris and vagina, so you become aroused more quickly and are more receptive to pleasure," says Lisa Masterson, an ob-gyn at Cedars-Sinai Medical Center in Los Angeles.

TO LOCATE YOUR PCs: The next time you're peeing, try stopping and then releasing your urine stream. Or lie back and insert one of your fingers into your vagina, then clamp your vaginal walls around it. Those babies are your PCs.

ONCE YOU'VE PINPOINTED YOUR PC MUSCLES, establish a routine where you do approximately 10 to 20 squeezes and releases at least three times daily, building up to holding each for 10 seconds. Total time spent: a mere 5 to 10 minutes a day.

Secret Times to Kegel Squeeze

When your car is stopped at a red light	Waiting for your microwave popcorn to finish popping
Every time you step into an elevator	During movie trailers
While in line to pay at the grocery store	When you're waiting for your computer to boot up
When you brush your teeth	During the time it takes for your coffee to brew

HOT TIP

Put your Kegel know-how to use during masturbation. Squeeze for a slow count of two, then release for two seconds. You'll notice your pleasurable sensations growing stronger and deeper with each flex of those PC muscles.

It pays to master the art of the tease.

How to Make a Man Ache for You All Day

▶ Now that you understand how important it is to get yourself in a sexy state of mind before hitting the sheets, it's time to turn your attention to the guy in your sights…and put him on a slow burn of desire. You see, men too can benefit from allowing frisky thoughts to fester. And you can help them along by providing the inspiration.

LUST-BUILDING TACTICS

A great way to launch your make-him-ache-campaign is by exploiting your guy's innately visual nature…and if you're together in the morning, that's a great time to start.

Now it's no secret that the sight of you naked will turn him on, but the trick to getting him so electrified that he'll pant with anticipation all day long is to make him think he's getting an accidental peep show. "It's more of a turn-on for a man to see a woman exposed, or even partially exposed, when he thinks he shouldn't be noticing," says Joan Elizabeth Lloyd, author of *The Perfect Orgasm*. Some ways to give your guy an "accidental" thrill:

■ Splash some water on your chest as you wash your face and act as if you have no idea that

Give him a sexy flash of flesh to trigger his primal urge to pursue you.

your nipples are torpedoing through your camisole.

■ Give him just a teasing peek of your naked bod by leaving the bathroom door open a crack so

he can catch of glimpse of you stepping out of the shower.

■ Hike your postshower towel up high enough to show just the bottom of your cheeks.

■ Feign a little helplessness and ask him to zip up your dress, revealing your bare back in the process.

■ Let him catch you caressing yourself. Just running your fingers lightly along your collarbone, smoothing body lotion on your arms, or slowly straightening your skirt over your hips with a downward stroke instantly draws a man's attention to your body. It may sound like a cheap ploy, but it works. "When you touch yourself, a guy subconsciously reads it as a cue that you want him to touch you too," explains sex coach Patti Britton, PhD, coauthor of *The Complete Idiot's Guide to Sensual Massage*. But whatever you do, don't let him get his hands on you yet! Men love the idea of a chase, so when you give him a flash of flesh or get "caught" touching yourself, it triggers his primal urge to pursue you.

Lusty Language

"Explicit language provokes an immediate lustful response in men," explains Patti Britton, PhD. Here's how to sneak saucy words into your conversations.

INSTEAD OF:	SAY:	EXAMPLE:
"I'd love"	"I'm hot for"	"I'm hot for a mojito right now."
"To die for"	"Pure ecstasy"	"That chocolate cake was pure ecstasy."
"Straight"	"Erect"	"My yoga instructor says that erect poses are the hardest."
"Raised"	"Aroused"	"That TV show's getting so much buzz. My interest is really aroused."

27

Supplying subtle sneak peeks of your body and drawing his attention to your curves will definitely entice your guy, but your mission here is to start him on a slow burn that will turn him into a towering inferno of desire.

So offer him a suggestive morning send-off when the two of you are parting ways. That brief moment is a great time to plant the seeds of passion, but most couples miss the opportunity because they let their good-byes become mechanical over time. Instead of giving him a quick peck when he's leaving for work, linger for at least 10 seconds, use a little tongue, and hint at what you'd do to him if you had more time by grabbing his butt with both hands. "Letting a man know you're hot for him ramps up his own libido because learning that your sex drive is in high gear is a turn-on in itself," says David Weiss, PhD, a board-certified sex therapist practicing in Massachusetts.

Describe something sexy, such as the new lingerie you just bought.

SEDUCE HIM ALL DAY—FROM AFAR

Once a guy's interest is piqued, the goal becomes keeping him hooked. And thankfully, it doesn't require a lot of heavy lifting because you have other demands on your time—like your job! The trick: Make it a point to check in with the object of your lust during the day to ensure that he can't escape the sexy memory of you.

There was a time when a short-but-sweet phone call would be in order. But since you're a modern chick, why not use a modern mode of communication, such as a text message? Sending a text is the perfect way to perpetuate sexual energy because it allows you to be a little more brazen than you might be normally. Some hints for crafting an electronic note so electrifying that he'd drop his BlackBerry/Sidekick/Treo and bolt straight to your house if he could:

■ **Use sexy but coy phrases.** Double entendres such as "U up 4 fun? Cum over now" trigger instant male arousal since they hint that you want sex, without directly saying so.

■ **Sound impatient.** Using all caps for words like NOW sends the message that you want him…badly.

■ **Draw a dirty picture.** You know guys are visually driven, so describe something sexy, such as the skimpy bikini you tried on at lunchtime.

■ **Pay him a hot compliment.** Stroking his ego, especially when it comes to his bedroom talents, let's him know that you're climbing the walls thinking specifically about him.

RAMP UP YOUR TEASING SKILLS

As you've likely figured out by now, the art of seduction is just that—an art. And unlike the paint-by-number variation (a slick coat of makeup and scant clothes), seduction in its truest form is something that must be taught. And you're already well on your way to becoming a brilliant seductress since you've learned how to make a guy ache with anticipation. Now it's time to take your skills to the next level, which means discovering how to enchant the pants off a man. The great news here is that these powerful techniques—which employ both your body and your mind—work equally well on a guy you've known three minutes, three months, or three years.

SPORT SOME CLEAVAGE

If you're a chick, you have boobs. And whether you're an A cup or a double D, guys respond the same way: they stare, they grope, they write erotic poetry. Understanding the depth of this obsession requires a short lesson in evolution. Here goes: According to anthropologist Helen Fisher,

Sex Texts to Entice Him

I was a BAD GIRL and spent my lunch hour shopping. You can spank me later.

Had a stressful day. I NEED you to help me unwind. Wink, wink.

My roommate is out of town. Let's throw a party tonight—for two.

HOT kiss this a.m. Hope you can finish what you started...

Splurged at Victoria's Secret. A girl can't have too many lacy panties, can she?

No movies out I want to see. Other ideas for what we can do in the dark?

Your flirting will be more fruitful if you work your natural assets.

it confirms for him that he's wanted, which is the ultimate confidence booster," says relationship expert Gilda Carle, PhD, professor of psychology and communications at Mercy College, in Dobbs Ferry, New York. It also lets him know that

PhD, author of *Why We Love*, "Male primates know when females are ready to mate because the tissue around their genitals becomes large and engorged (and because they walk on all fours, their backsides are visible from the front). Because men can't see women's buttocks from the front, some scientists believe that fleshy breasts evolved to mimic them." Strange but true. If seducing someone is on your agenda, put your breasts to work. Big or small, they're the most readily available seduction tool you've got, sister.

"When a woman flirts with a man, it confirms for him that he's wanted, which is the ultimate confidence booster."

POUR ON THE CHARM

Running a close second to your smokin' physical assets is your dazzling personality. And that's what truly seals the deal on a guy's longing for you—really, it is. But before you can shine, you have to make him feel like a rock star. "When a man is flirted with,

he's on your sexual radar. If you're in a long-term relationship, it's smart to heed this advice too. "When you stop trying to seduce your guy, it sends a not-so-great message—'I don't need to impress you now that I have you on speed dial'—which makes him feel undesirable," says Carle. So whether you have

just locked eyes with a hot stranger or want to make your steady man know you hunger for him, these libido-spiking ideas can serve as your inspiration:

■ Give him a long once-over from head to toe, then bring your eyes back up to his. Smile ever-so-slightly to let him know you like what you see.

■ Pull your hair loose from a ponytail holder or clip so he can watch your touchable tresses fall around your face.

used to focusing on movement.

■ Dip your finger into your dessert (order something with whipped cream), put it in your mouth, then slowly pull it out while eyeing your guy.

BREAKING THE TOUCH BARRIER

Flirting physically is, in some ways, more important than just enticing with words, because breaking the physical boundary is what sends the message

Making subtle physical contact is what sends the message to a guy that you want to sleep with him.

■ Cross your legs and slowly move your top foot in circles. His eyes will be drawn to your gorgeous gams since men are

loud and clear that you want to sleep with a guy. So look for opportunities to make contact. And since a guy you've been with for a while isn't going to get all hot and bothered if you grab his hand while you're walking down the street, the key to being touchy-flirty is to do it in unexpected ways. A few suggestions:

■ During conversation, touch his knee or hand for emphasis.

■ Say that you're trying out a new perfume, then expose your neck and ask his opinion.

■ Ask him if it's hot (or cold) in the room and put his hands on your cheeks or neck for a temperature check.

■ Tell him you're an amateur palm reader, then take his hand and trace the creases.

■ Wonder aloud about what time it is, then grab his wrist and pull it toward you to get a glance at his watch.

■ Slip off one shoe and play footsie with him under the table at a dimly lit restaurant.

HOME AND ALONE... WITH HIM

Good job—you've now meandered successfully down the passion path. The end result? You've created a sky-high level of sexual intensity. But there does come a time when you want to get down to the action you've both been waiting for—and guess what? That time is right now. ■

Turn Your Bedroom Into a Sexy Sanctuary

1 **BANISH CLUTTER.** Your bedroom should be a refuge from the outside world. But that's not a possibility if it's filled with stacks of laundry and file folders.

2 **KEEP LIGHTING SOFT AND SEXY.** Nix harsh overheads in favor of table lamps with colored bulbs (no higher than 60 watts) in a soft, flattering shade, such as pink. Of course, the glow of candlelight is the best illumination for each other's bods.

3 **PERFUME YOUR ROOM.** A bedside essential: incense or a scented candle in a fragrance you find relaxing. Some suggestions: lavender, musk, jasmine, and amber.

4 **INVEST IN TOP-NOTCH LINENS.** It makes sense to splurge a bit on great sheets (look for a thread count of at least 300). They're like a sexy outfit you slip into every night.

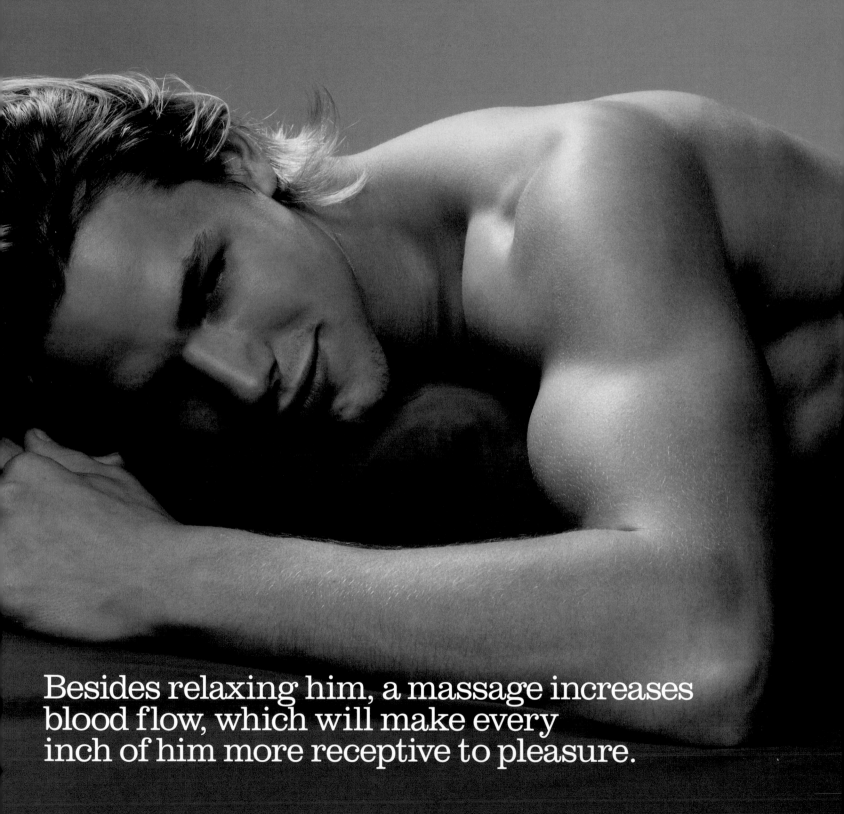

Besides relaxing him, a massage increases blood flow, which will make every inch of him more receptive to pleasure.

Treat Him to an Erotic Massage

▶ When you want to be intimate but don't want to dive right into bed, consider giving your man a sensual rubdown. Massage can bring couples closer because it lets you exercise your nurturing side, explains Patti Britton, PhD, author of *The Complete Idiot's Guide to Sensual Massage*, and he's letting his guard down by surrendering his body to you. But be careful where your fingers wander—his penis is to be ignored for now. By concentrating on his other body parts, he'll have a chance to experience delicious new sensations.

First, have him strip down (the most you should be wearing is a sexy bra-and-pantie set). Make sure the room is warm enough to be comfortable naked—72 degrees is a good temperature.

Then, warm a light lotion in your hands. Since you're planning to have sex afterward (no point in being coy, is there?), make sure the product is water-based, since oil-based lubricants break down condoms. You can find massage oils made especially for sensual rubdowns in novelty shops, on-line, and even in a drugstore. Tell your man to lie facedown with a loose sheet beneath him.

Bear in mind that any feeling, no matter how good, gets old if you overdo it. That's why *how* you touch a man is just as important as *where* you touch him. Vary the amount of pressure and the kind of strokes you use: Knead his inner thighs like a loaf of bread; press your knuckles into his lower back to create a gentle ribbing effect; use the side of your fist to pummel his butt cheeks lightly. Professional masseuses have a stroke secret

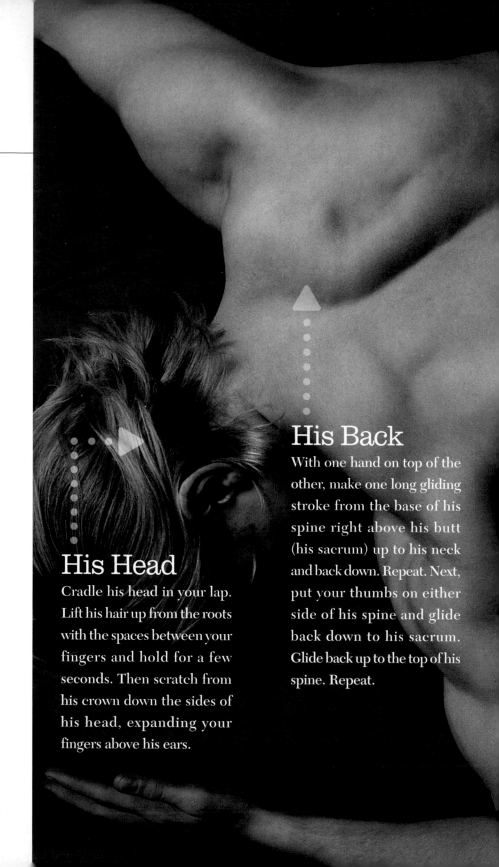

His Head

Cradle his head in your lap. Lift his hair up from the roots with the spaces between your fingers and hold for a few seconds. Then scratch from his crown down the sides of his head, expanding your fingers above his ears.

His Back

With one hand on top of the other, make one long gliding stroke from the base of his spine right above his butt (his sacrum) up to his neck and back down. Repeat. Next, put your thumbs on either side of his spine and glide back down to his sacrum. Glide back up to the top of his spine. Repeat.

Along His Sides

Beneath this soft run of skin are tension-filled muscles. Place your hands on either side of his waist, fingers pointing up. Using light pressure, slide them up and down his torso.

His Buttocks

When a man's turned on, his body releases feel-good chemicals called endorphins, making stinging butt slaps feel like pleasurable pats. Give his buns a mini-massage with a firm kneading motion. Another cheek-pleasing technique: Run your nails along his backside and tickle the spot where his back and butt meet.

The Crease in His Thigh

The area between his torso and legs is a covert hot spot. Press your thumbs delicately into one crease, massaging your way from one side to the other.

Ask him to flip over so he is lying faceup. ▶

His Inner Arms

This thin-skinned zone contains a lot of nerve endings, so it's receptive to the lightest touch. To turn him on without venturing into ticklish territory, run your nails in long strokes up and down the front of the muscle.

His Nipples

Believe it or not, men's nipples can be as sensitive as yours are. Lightly brush them with the backs of your fingers, then softly run the palms of your hands over each one in a circular motion.

HOT TIP
Try not to speak while giving your guy a massage—talking distracts him from feeling every shock wave coursing through his body.

His Treasure Trail

Trace a vertical line from his navel down to where his pubic hair begins. Massaging this area encourages blood flow to his entire pelvic region (don't be surprised if he gets an erection; just do your best not to pounce on it). Now change directions by tracing a horizontal line across his abdomen from one hip to the other. Imagine that there are 10 dots along this line, five on each side of his navel spaced an equal distance apart. Gently rub each point for three to five seconds.

we're gonna let you in on: They never take their hands off a client's body. Removing them— even for a moment—disrupts that skin-on-skin connection. That said, guys rarely admit their discomfort, so pay attention to physical cues that you're massaging him too roughly— such as open eyes or a clenched jaw. If you spot these, lighten up a little.

One last thing to remember: The point of an erotic massage is to stimulate, not sedate, so be sure to use more than your hands. Lean over him and let your hair graze his back; rub your breasts over his body; warm his skin with your breath. These techniques are just suggestions since you should feel free to explore your man's body any way you please—let his moans of pleasure serve as your guide. ■

Bed-Me Beauty

▶ Instinctively, you know that when you look your best you're more apt to approach—or be approached by—a guy. But there's actually some serious science behind how your outward beauty correlates to your ability to seduce.

Experts have discovered that your allure starts with projecting a healthy vibe. "If you have a healthful glow, you're sending a message to men that your hormones and other chemicals are in balance, which means you're good mate material," explains anthropologist Helen Fisher, PhD, author of *Why We Love*. Learn what guys are innately attracted to, then employ these easy beauty moves to maximize your appeal.

Certain beauty tricks can enhance your powers of seduction.

WIDE EYES

From an evolutionary standpoint, big, bright eyes have been one of a woman's most reliably potent seduction tools. "Historically, when a woman had large, glistening eyes, it was almost like she was wearing a sign that said, 'I'm fertile—I'd make a great mate,'" says Fisher.

Fast-forward to the present: While guys may not necessarily be looking for a mate to repro-

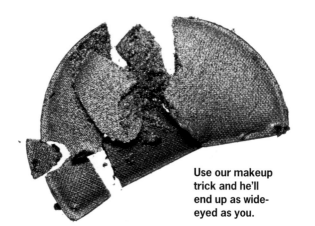

Use our makeup trick and he'll end up as wide-eyed as you.

top and bottom lash lines from the middle of the lid to just past the outer corner of the eye, he says. Then use a cotton swab to blend and smudge the line. Sweep a shimmery shadow (the same hue as your liner) over your lid, he says.

From an evolutionary standpoint, big, bright eyes have been one of a woman's most potent seduction tools.

These are part of your sex-goddess arsenal.

duce with, they're drawn on a subconscious level to seek out a woman who gives off a healthy and fertile aura.

BEAUTY TRICKS To widen your eyes, play up the outer corners, says celebrity makeup artist Troy Surrat. With a black or brown pencil, trace along the

Next, dab a champagne-colored pencil over the inner corner of your eye, right near your tear duct. Use an eyelash curler on your lashes, then layer on two coats of jet-black mascara. To complete the look, apply one more coat of mascara but only to the outermost lashes, advises Surrat.

"Though no two women smell exactly the same, almost all possess a scent that's a combination of sweet and musky that men find incredibly sexy."

BEAUTY TRICKS For an easy way to seduce him, pinpoint a perfume that mimics a woman's natural scent (i.e., that sweet and musky blend). "Go for fragrances that mix sweet notes like vanilla and rose with deeper, musky ones like sandalwood," says perfumer Virginia Bonofiglio, adjunct professor at the Fashion Institute of Technology in New York City.

Don't overwhelm him with a cloud of perfume. Instead, apply just a subtle spritz only to your pulse points—the insides of the wrists, insides of the elbows, the backs of the knees, and the neck.

A COME-HITHER SCENT

Fragrance is an important turn-him-on tool, but not all scents sync up with men's subconscious cravings. Guys tend to gravitate toward something that enhances your already alluring natural scent. Says Fisher,

43

She has the kind of healthy glow guys go gaga for.

Hey C:

SUPERSHINY HAIR

Anthropologists don't know why thick, continually growing hair evolved, says Fisher. No other mammal has it, so it is generally thought that it's for signaling a mate. But lustrous hair, specifically, is an advertisement that you're in optimal health, and "men naturally gravitate toward women who have the potential to bear healthy babies," she says.

BEAUTY TRICKS Apply a shine-enhancing volumizer to towel-dried hair from roots to ends for a glossy and full-of-body effect. For thick-looking locks, finger-tousle while you blow-dry; then, when your do is almost dry, use a brush to style it in place. Once dry, use a lightweight finishing spray; anything heavier can dull your mane. ■

45

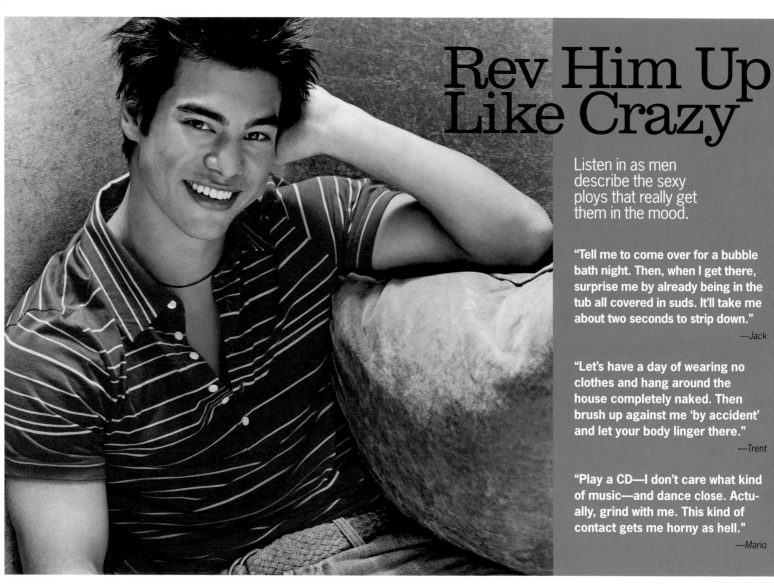

Rev Him Up Like Crazy

Listen in as men describe the sexy ploys that really get them in the mood.

"Tell me to come over for a bubble bath night. Then, when I get there, surprise me by already being in the tub all covered in suds. It'll take me about two seconds to strip down."
—Jack

"Let's have a day of wearing no clothes and hang around the house completely naked. Then brush up against me 'by accident' and let your body linger there."
—Trent

"Play a CD—I don't care what kind of music—and dance close. Actually, grind with me. This kind of contact gets me horny as hell."
—Mario

"I love it when you run your fingers through my chest hair or leg hair. All those follicles stand up and notice." —Pat

"Cook for me wearing nothing but sexy underwear. All I'll be able to think about is how badly I want to have you for dessert." —Billy

"My girl once dragged me to a furniture store to buy a nightstand. By the time we brought it home, I was in a bad mood. Then I opened the drawer and saw lube and a vibrator. My mood improved instantly." —Art

"Once, my office phone rang, and when I answered, I heard my girlfriend at home moaning about how good it feels to touch herself." —Erik

"Seeing a woman's lips glide over the neck of a beer bottle always makes me think of her mouth on me." —Lamar

"My ex-girlfriend brilliantly teased me by stopping by my job one afternoon with her blouse partly unbuttoned, knowing I couldn't do anything about it." —Sam

"Watching a woman do yoga is the hottest thing you can do without actually touching each other." —Kirk

"While we're having a completely normal conversation, casually mention you're not wearing underwear and I swear I won't stop thinking about it until I can see for myself." —James

"A chick I dated once had a messenger send me a letter at work. It was a very intricate diagram of her body with details of what I should do with each part." —Oscar

"A girl pal of mine brought over one of her friends for drinks. The friend said that she was on the prowl. That kind of confidence got me thinking about going down on her for the rest of the night." —Sean

"When we're out having dinner, rub and touch me under the table. It's a turn-on to know that other people may be watching us be naughty." —Simon

She found
the man of
her dreams—
literally.

Decoding Your Sex Dreams

▶ At some point, everyone has gotten laid in la-la land. And aside from being a naughty bedtime treat, sizzling visions can offer a fascinating peek into your psyche. (There's a reason why it popped into your head.) "Sexual dreams reveal your desires and anxieties," says dream-analysis expert Gillian Holloway, PhD, author of *Erotic Dreams*. "Your subconscious uses these raw, lustful situations to sort out emotions you may not be confronting in waking life."

Something else to keep in mind: Often your dirtiest scenes aren't about sex at all, while your "innocent" imaginings are loaded with sexual meaning. Yes, it's confusing—that's why we've dissected some of the most common dirty dreams for you.

HAVING SEX FOR ALL TO SEE

Right in the middle of a XXX romp, you suddenly realize you're onstage or in a roomful of people...with all eyes on you. "If the crowd makes you self-conscious, you could be worried that people are gossiping about your relationship," says Holloway. Think about it: Are you afraid your pals don't like your boyfriend? Did you start dating before he completely disentangled from a relationship with someone else? On the other hand, if being in the spotlight felt deliciously naughty, it means you have a hankering to flaunt your sizzling sex life to the world.

YOU SHAGGED YOUR BOSS

In some cases, dreaming of having sex with a higher-up suggests that you long to have a sexual relationship with a powerful person, says Gayle Delaney, PhD, author

Dreams of getting it on with a higher-up could hint at a longing for power.

of *All About Dreams*. But usually, it has more to do with admiration. "Many women have this dream after receiving a promotion," says Holloway. "You probably aspire to achieve the level of success that your boss has," she says.

YOU GOT IT ON WITH A GIRL

If you've never been with a woman, you may wonder if some latent bisexual urges are surfacing, but that's not likely. "Usually, when straight women have same-sex dreams, they're doing it with a woman they look up to," says Delaney. It's not that you secretly want her body; it's more likely that you have a platonic girl crush. You may love her style or killer personality, so you dreamed about getting intimate with her to feel close to her fabulousness.

YOU HAD A RENDEZVOUS WITH A CELEB

"People who are sexually active but aren't currently having sex—whether it's due to their partner's being away or a recent

Sleeping your way to the top just took on a whole new meaning.

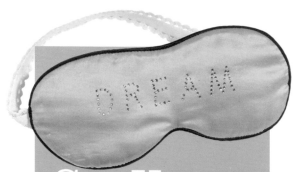

Sex Up Your Dreams

Kill the lights and attempt this sensual sleep strategy from *Secrets of Dreams*, by Caro Ness. First, settle down as if you're going to sleep, relaxing every muscle in your body. Then focus all of your mind's attention on the area around your genitals.

Keeping your eyes shut and your eye muscles relaxed, direct your mental energy downward, feeling the blood circulate. Then "look" into the darkness of your eyelids. It may take a few tries, but according to Ness, concentrating on the most erotic part of your body before drifting off to sleep can cause intensely sexual images to pop up in your nighttime reveries.

breakup—often have celebrity-centric sex dreams," says psychologist Patricia Farrell, PhD, author of *How to Be Your Own Therapist*. In other words, you're subconsciously craving what you're missing: sex. And your famous bed buddy is bringing that purely physical urge to the forefront.

You'll never look at your cute cousin the same way again.

YOU BEDDED A RELATIVE

It's so cringeworthy you can barely think about it, right? Well, you can relax. Freaky familial fantasies rarely have anything to do with incest. "They usually have to do with personality types that you encounter in your life that remind you of your family," Holloway says. "For instance, if your brother used to tease you as a kid, and now your guy jokes around a lot, you might dream about sleeping with your brother because they share that trait."

YOU SLEPT WITH YOUR FRIEND'S MAN

Just because you dove under the sheets with him in a spicy slumber-induced fantasy doesn't mean you've hatched a subversive plot to steal a pal's boyfriend. "Often a dream will 'borrow' a situation from a friend's life," says Holloway. "If your pal has a funnier or more successful partner than you do, the dream may be suggesting that you'd like to be with someone like him or you'd like more excitement, empathy, or laughter in your life."

Obviously, there wasn't a bedroom available.

DIRTY DREAMS

By age 45, 37 percent of women have experienced an orgasm during a sex dream.

SOURCE: THE KINSEY INSTITUTE FOR RESEARCH IN SEX, GENDER, AND REPRODUCTION

obstacle you're trying to overcome, such as living in different cities, or even just that you're unsure what the future holds.

CHEATING ON YOUR MAN

It's pretty unsettling to imagine getting busy behind your guy's back. "You usually dream of sleeping with someone else soon after taking a major relationship step, like getting engaged," says Holloway. "Any uneasiness about making such a huge life change (which is normal, by the way) can manifest in your dreams." It doesn't mean you have regrets; you're just experiencing valid concerns, like that you're missing out on other potential mates or you'll one day discover he's not right for you.

THERE'S NO PLACE TO GET BUSY

You're on a hunt for a place to have sex with your man, but problems arise that make hooking up impossible. "This suggests a loss of intimacy between you and him," explains Holloway.

"Women tend to have this dream just before or just after a breakup." Although you've struggled to make it work, something—like mismatched goals—has prevented it.

However, if you and your man are happily coupled, the dream may indicate that there's an

53

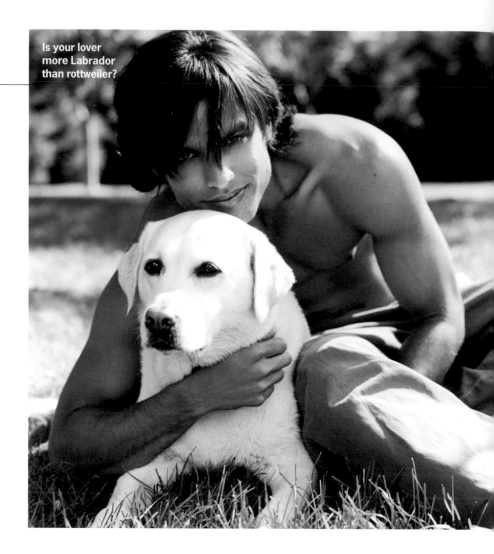

Is your lover more Labrador than rottweiler?

On the flip side: "If your man's the unfaithful one in your dream, ask yourself if you're resenting him for some reason," suggests Holloway. "This dream can expose feelings of emotional abandonment—perhaps he's working a lot or you're more serious about your relationship than he is."

AN ANIMAL ENCOUNTER

No, we're not talking about bestiality! When a gorgeous, shiny-coated stallion makes a late-night appearance, it suggests you're getting in touch with your wild side. "Galloping on a horse symbolizes that you feel alive, liberated, and in control sexually," says Holloway. The rhythm and speed of riding feels similar to the steady tempo of sex (as does any rhythmic motion, such as swinging), and being atop a huge, powerful animal echoes the exhilaration of being with a man. Hello, they call them studs for a reason.

Not all animal-related scenarios are positive though. If scaly reptiles give you the heebie-jeebies, then a snake nightmare (talk about phallic!) points to worries you have, possibly about sex, according to Patricia Garfield, PhD, author of *The Universal Dream Key*. "Also, some people connect snakes with being sneaky," adds Garfield. "This dream could signal you've subconsciously picked up on the fact that a guy you've been seeing is using you for sex or hiding something about his sexual past." Call it intuition…in fantasy form.

FLYING THROUGH THE SKY

Often when you dream that you're soaring through the air, you've recently had a mind-bending romp in real life. "This euphoric feeling is called ecstatic flight, and it's analogous to an orgasm," says Holloway. "Flying dreams are usually about getting some freedom in your life and being as unfet-

tered as you possibly can. The dream could be telling you that stepping out of your sexual comfort zone is allowing you to break free of your fears and insecurities and that you should move forward with your adventurousness."

YOU SUDDENLY HAVE SUPER-LONG LOCKS

Envisioning a Rapunzel-like mane while mid-REM serves as a carnal wake-up call—you have been putting sex on the back burner and are ready to devote due energy to satisfying your erotic drive. "Long hair represents sensuality and femininity, encouraging you to let your natural impulses rule," says Holloway. So stop snoozing on your sex life and actively seek out the kind of action you've only, uh, dreamed of. ∎

More Ways to Encourage Spicier Sleep Sessions

Wear something seductive to bed, like silk lingerie, to make you feel sensual.

Consciously tell yourself that you want to have an erotic dream. Then completely relax.

Watch a steamy movie or read a lusty novel prebed.

Before nodding off, masturbate but stop short of orgasm so you drift off in an aroused state.

55

Guys have a reputation for speeding through foreplay, but there are times when women rush it too, like in a new relationship when they don't yet feel comfortable expressing how much of a warm-up they need. Or later, when they've eased into a sexual routine (okay, rut) with a man and tend to dive right into intercourse, dispensing with the passionate preamble. But foreplay is something that really shouldn't be rushed (save for the occasional quickie!), because taking the time to heat up your body—and his—greatly increases the likelihood that you'll both experience incredibly intense orgasms.

And there's something else you should keep in mind: Foreplay can be pretty freakin' pleasurable all on its own. In fact, engaging in presex activity isn't so much about delaying gratification as it is about drawing out the fun.

In the following pages, we'll tell you everything you need to know: his biggest turn-ons, how to teach him what works for you, some amazing oral-sex tricks, great ways to use sex toys, and finally, an easy tutorial on that ultraintimate act known as 69. After sampling the tricks we've amassed here, you'll never rush through foreplay again.

eplay foreplay foreplay foreplay foreplay foreplay

The Kind of Kissing Men Crave

His knees
are buckling
right now.

▶ It's time to bust a widely held myth: Contrary to popular belief, guys *do* like making out. Sure, they may sometimes treat kissing like it's a brief, obligatory stop on the way to a much more interesting destination, but when reminded—by you and your lips, of course—how hot kissing can be, they will slow down...and beg for more. And that's what you want—to get a guy craving more of you.

But we're going to do better than that. You're about to learn how to make a man moan with the touch of your mouth alone. The secret is knowing how to "grow" a kiss. That's when you mesh your lips with his in a slow, sensuous way and then progress to being more playful and, finally, more aggressive. Here, kisses that will rock his world:

GREAT BASIC KISS

STEP 1

First, kiss your lover's face all over. Start out with dry, baby pecks on his eyebrows, chin, and cheeks. Then, trace the outline of his lips with the tip of your tongue. When you get to his mouth, don't plunge your tongue in. Instead, slowly exert a little more pressure with your lips and insert your tongue just beyond

When you can feel him quivering with anticipation, slip him the tongue with a lot of wetness to amp his excitement.

his parted lips. Entice him by pulling your tongue back altogether and sucking gently on his bottom lip to create an enveloping, pulsating sensation.

STEP 2

When you can almost feel him quivering with anticipation, slip him the tongue with a lot of

wetness to increase his sexual excitement…and yours. You might want to tease the tip of your tongue against his, since that's the most sensitive area, then bring the kiss to its pinnacle by alternating between lightly sucking on his tongue and moving your tongue freely around his mouth.

STEP 3

Use your hands by gently tugging on his hair, caressing his face, and lightly stroking his thighs while you're in mid-kiss. If you really want to work him into a lather, sigh aloud while you do all these things.

That lip-lock is guaranteed to make any man's toes curl. But you don't have to stop there: If you're game, try this collection

of smooches that are so creative and captivating, we like to refer to it as the Kissing Kama Sutra.

The Suction Seduction

To start, tilt your head up slightly and place your lips around his upper lip as he does the same to your lower lip. Alternate soft nuzzles with tender sucking. Then switch positions so you take in his lower lip. Trade off a few times, then part your lips and take his entire mouth in your own. Suck gently, and then let him do the same to you.

What makes this move so killer is that the delicate suction draws more blood to the surface of the lips, making them hyper-sensitive to each other's touch, says William Cane, author of *The Art of Kissing*.

The Hot-and-Cold Kiss

Start by sipping a heated drink. Let the liquid warm your mouth, then plant a red-hot French kiss on your guy. While he's catching his breath, take a mouthful of something cold, like ice cream, to cool your kisser down, and repeat the pucker. "By varying the temperature, you're activating two separate sets of nerve endings," Cane explains.

The Naughty Nibble

Use your teeth on every part of your guy's highly biteable bod:

This beverage can improve your kissing technique.

Plant your lips under his earlobe, and as you work your way down his neck, gently take his flesh between your front teeth, tug just a fraction of an inch, then release. While this may strike you as a bit ferocious, you should know that these little love bites drive most men wild. (Quick biological fact: As you

what's coming next, which forces his whole body into a state of excitement.

Around the World

Guys already go gaga for French kisses, so when you take charge and really dominate his mouth with yours, he'll get into it even

then along the outer gums. Drop down and trace a tantalizing trail along his lower gums. To finish off, twirl your tongue a complete 360 degrees around his. This is a powerful move because you're stimulating all sorts of unexplored territory.

The Tongue Twister

Every thrust your man makes during intercourse bumps his pleasure up a few notches. Give him a mouth-to-mouth version of that in-and-out action and it'll create a similar thrill—in large part *because* it mimics sex. To do it, stick your tongue out of your mouth and slide it between his loosely closed lips. Slip it slowly in and out. (If you whip this baby out when you're making love, you'll cause twice the fireworks.) ∎

"By varying the temperature between hot and cold, you're activating two separate sets of nerve endings."

become aroused, your body releases endorphins, which block pain receptors and turn normally stinging sensations into pleasurably erotic ones.) And if you alternate light pecks with nibbles, he won't know

more. Run the firm tip of your tongue along the middle of the roof of his mouth, then back toward his throat. Let your tongue soften and slink to the side, prowling its way slowly around his teeth—first on the inside,

Yes, M could
also stand for
moan zone.

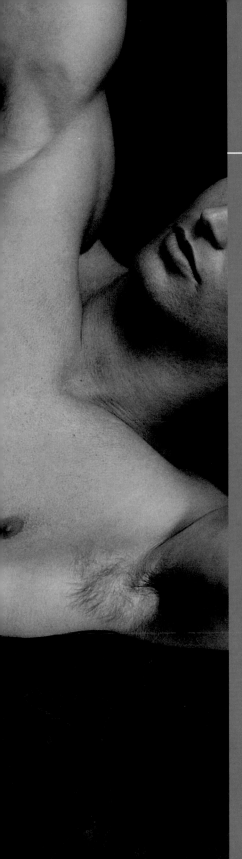

Master His M Zone

▶ When it comes to pleasuring themselves, men usually head straight for their penises. (Hey, it's easy access.) But what makes foreplay with you (followed, of course, by the main event) so exciting for him is the very sensual and circuitous path you take him on. One possible route traverses a territory we've named his M zone: This represents the M-shaped trail you make on his body when you touch him in this densely nerve-packed region between his upper thighs and lower stomach. Moving both of your hands in tandem (one on each leg), we suggest you navigate the region using the following techniques.

STEP 1
TANTALIZE HIS THIGHS

When you're on the bed, have him lie on his back with his legs spread about 6 inches apart. Either kneel beside his bod or gently straddle him, with your butt on his lower thighs. Rub your hands together briskly to warm them up a little, then rest them palm down on each of his upper thighs. Moving slowly, knead the outside of his thighs only and, with light contact at first, build up gradually to the point where you're using plenty of pressure.

Gradually slide your hands up and down and side to side over this outer upper-thigh area,

Don't be afraid of getting too his quads—are among a man's

mixing up your strokes, going from long, smooth ones to circular, kneading motions. Don't be afraid of getting too rough, since these muscles—his quads—are among a man's strongest and thickest. Switch to softer, lighter, feathery strokes as you move closer to his inner thighs, where the nerve endings become more sensitive. In this region, he can be stimulated by the slightest touch. Warning: He may also become ticklish, so stay attuned to his reactions and facial expressions as you go.

STEP 2
SLIDE UP TO HIS HIP BONES

Chances are, he may become erect from all that heavy-duty thigh stimulation, but ignore his hard-on for now (we know that's not an easy assignment, but do your best!). Simply move both

connective penile tissue exists in the thin stretch of skin just inside both of his hip bones, so a lighter touch is absolutely necessary. Work this area with some TLC: Make gentle circles with the tips of your fingers, then switch to light, swirling motions with your tongue. (You can also surprise him by rubbing a furry scarf or even your hair up along the area.) For an added thrill, reach under his

rough, since these muscles—strongest and thickest.

of your hands upward toward his hips, stopping right above and inside the hip bones.

Now it's time to seriously ease up with your hand action—the last thing you want to do is put any pressure on his bones. That's because supersensitive

body and drag your fingers upward and across his tush, moving very slowly toward the base of his spine. "The tailbone is filled with nerve endings, so gently massaging this region will feel great to him," says Patti Britton, PhD.

STEP 3
AROUSE HIS "ALMOST" AREA

With a tender touch, slide your fingers diagonally inward, just above where his lower abs end and his pubic hair starts. "He's going to assume you're headed for his penis at any moment, but prolonging that move is ultra-tantalizing for him," explains sex therapist Sandor Gardos, PhD, founder of MyPleasure.com. Try blowing on the area lightly, segueing into long sensual licks across this stretch of flesh.

The key to pushing him over the edge is to take your time. In fact, this M-zone journey is the perfect prelude to giving a man a hand job or oral sex. ∎

Things are about to get very steamy.

Wet 'n' Wild Fun

▶ A soak in the bath always feels incredible, and usually, taking one is a relaxing solo pursuit. But the sensual thrills quadruple when you invite your man in for some rub-a-dub action. Though having intercourse in a tub is tricky because the water washes away lubrication, indulging in a soapy sexcapade can be the ultimate foreplay. These moves will fog up the mirror—fast.

THE SULTRY SPONGE BATH

Start by peeling off each other's clothes, then slide into a warm tub with your guy sitting behind you. Take turns slowly lathering each other up with a soft natural sea sponge or a mesh sponge. Then, with his hand on top of yours, start tracing slow, sexy circles around your breasts, belly, and inner thighs.

Next, guide his hand from the base of your vulva to the top and back down again. "This sponge bath stimulates highly sensitive parts of the vulva that are often neglected outside the tub," says Ian Kerner, PhD, author of *He Comes Next*. Once you've established a slow north-south rhythm, let his hands take over.

But before you get too hot and bothered, switch places. Drag the sudsy sponge from his chest down to his abs and then gently run it up and down his penis. The slick, warm feeling will create a toe-curling sensation for him.

Have him change the settings, working from a delicate spray to a pulsating rhythm.

LUSTY UNDERWATER LOTUS

Facing each other, wrap your legs around his back. Slide one hand down his belly and gently massage his testicles—think tickle, not tug. "Cup them in the palms of your hands and graze them with your fingertips like a little octopus," says Kerner.

SHOWERHEAD BLASTOFF

Start draining the tub as he turns on the shower to tantalize you with its warm stream. (If your shower has weak water pressure, you'll need a handheld showerhead to get the full effect.)

With your guy standing, lie back facing the showerhead with your legs splayed. Angle your body so the water sprays

These guys should cover their eyes!

down directly on your genitalia. Have him change the settings, working from a delicate spray to a pleasurably pulsating rhythm. "Just avoid directly spraying the clitoris, because the pressure may be too much for that sensitive spot," says Kerner. Once he brings you to the thigh-quivering brink, towel off and slip in between cool, crisp sheets together. ∎

Waterproof Playthings

To make your booty session a little more exciting, consider bringing a watersafe sex toy into the tub with you. You can find a surprisingly wide variety of them at online adult boutiques, such as MyPleasure.com. A few fun examples:

PASSION LILY
Use this multispeed vibrator, which is shaped like a blooming flower, for clitoral stimulation. It's nubbed specifically for that purpose.

RUBBA DUCKY
For grown-ups only, this cute bath buddy is a great tool to use for an allover (and we mean allover) massage.

JACK RABBIT
The ol' classic is now H₂Ohhh safe.

NAUGHTY SPONGE
This vibrating sponge stimulates your sexiest parts.

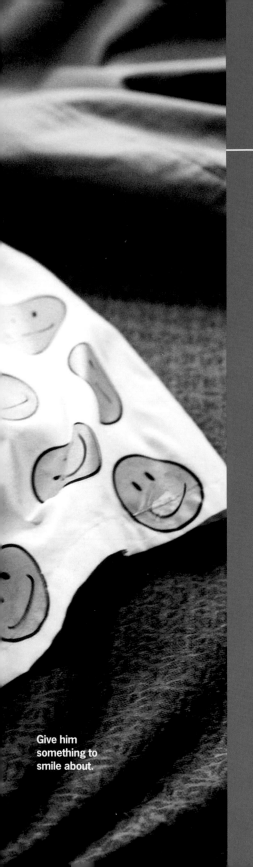

Give him something to smile about.

Become a Penis Genius

▶ As you know, men are well acquainted with their penises—much more so than most women are with their vaginas (we'll get to that later). So to be a truly talented lover—one who can rival the pleasure he can give himself—you have to sharpen your knowledge of his private parts. Don't worry—we're not going to subject you to a detailed anatomy lesson here. But you will learn some surprising stuff about how a guy's erotic equipment works. And we'll tell you how to use that juicy info to thrill the hell out of him. After this tutorial, you may actually know more about his member than he does!

For starters, what you see is not *all* that you get. "Around 50 percent of a guy's penis is internal," says Laurence Levine, MD, director of the Male Sexual Function and Fertility Program at Rush University Medical Center in Chicago. "It reaches way back to the pelvic bone."

THRILL-HIM TIP Tantalize his perineum, the patch of skin (it measures about 1 to 2 inches) between the scrotum and the anus. By pressing there, you'll indirectly massage the internal

Alternate rubbing the perineum in circles and pressing in on it with a pumping motion.

nerve system of his penis. Try this: During a hand job or oral sex, bend your index and middle fingers at the first two knuckles on one hand so they look like knees, suggests certified sex educator Lou Paget, author of *The Great Lover Playbook*.

Then, using the flat midsection of those bent fingers, alternate rubbing the perineum in a circular motion and pressing in on it with a pumping motion using varying pressure. If you plan to take him all the way to climax (and hey, why not?), press the

perineum more firmly as he's peaking to intensify his orgasm.

Another anatomical point of interest is the penis's hidden pleasure ring. It's located on the underside of the ridge where the head meets the shaft and it is jam-packed with nerve endings. Moreover, it is intensely receptive to touch. The V-shaped notch that interrupts this magic ridge is called the frenulum and it is also a major male hot spot.

Uncircumsized men have pleasure advantages— there are loads of nerve endings in the foreskin.

THRILL-HIM TIP While performing oral sex on him, alternate between sucking his shaft and running your tongue back and forth along the ridge. Or during manual manipulation, lubricate your thumb pad and make circular motions with it on the frenulum while constantly moving your free hand up and down the shaft. Yes, it takes a little coordination,

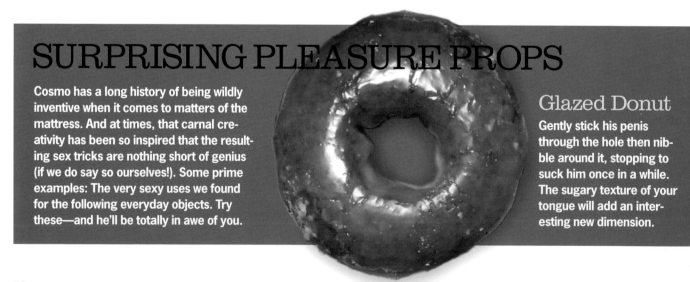

SURPRISING PLEASURE PROPS

Cosmo has a long history of being wildly inventive when it comes to matters of the mattress. And at times, that carnal creativity has been so inspired that the resulting sex tricks are nothing short of genius (if we do say so ourselves!). Some prime examples: The very sexy uses we found for the following everyday objects. Try these—and he'll be totally in awe of you.

Glazed Donut

Gently stick his penis through the hole then nibble around it, stopping to suck him once in a while. The sugary texture of your tongue will add an interesting new dimension.

but as the saying goes, practice makes perfect.

Here's something you might not be aware of: Uncircumcised men have certain pleasure advantages. The reason is that there are loads of nerve endings in the foreskin tissue, so for the 26 percent of American men ages 18 to 59 who are uncut, touching this area the right way can feel erotic, according to psychologist and sex therapist Howard Devore, PhD. If your guy is one of the majority of U.S. men who are circumcised, fear not: We have a simple sex trick that can mimic the foreskin effect we're about to describe.

THRILL-HIM TIP Before he's completely hard, slowly slide his foreskin up over the head of his penis, then back again. This motion hits all the sensitive parts of his penis. Don't be afraid to use some pressure. If he's circumcised, give him a "faux foreskin." "Just wrap a section of your own hair around his rod, making twisting motions as you work your hair up and down the ridge of his penis," says Paget. The silky strands will mimic the same feel-good friction of a foreskin. Got short hair? Substitute a soft swatch of fabric, like velvet. The possibilities are limited only by your creativity. ∎

String of Pearls

Wrap a strand of well-lubricated pearls (fake ones actually work best) around your hands, then move them up and down his penis, letting the pearls roll and slide against the head.

Hair Scrunchie

Once he's erect, wrap the scrunchie around the base of his testicles and his penis (twice if it's too loose). It needs to be tight, but not uncomfortable. That extra squeeze at the base of his genitals keeps blood trapped inside his erection, which causes pleasurable pressure during manual and oral sex.

Assure him he's in good hands.

More Secrets to Penis Pleasuring

▶ Just when you thought you knew all there was to know about satisfying and gratifying your man with your penis-handling prowess, we have more to share. It's an endlessly fascinating topic, don't you think? What you're about to learn now is that there are certain pleasure principles that are guaranteed to drive any guy out of his mind with delight—call them the secrets of sexual touch. They go like this....

1

SECRET

WHEN IN DOUBT, SQUEEZE HARDER

The amount of hands-on pressure that would make you say "Ouch" will likely make him say "Ooooh, yeah." Men's skin tends to be thicker, plus their nerve endings aren't as close to the skin's surface as women's are, so what might seem overly aggressive to you probably feels just right to him. It's time to show him what you've got.

Go beyond using your fingertips and grip his penis shaft with a firm, encompassing, full handhold. He'll love the fact that you feel comfortable taking control of his body. Then slide your fist up and down his shaft using twice the level of pressure you would normally

apply if you were holding his hand. Slather on lots of water-based lubricant—it enables greater ease of motion and cuts down on irritating friction. Start off slow, working up to a vigorous jerking rhythm. Ask him which speed he prefers and at what pressure, or you'll know you've found the right speed and grip if you feel his penis getting more and more engorged.

Knowledge is power. Ask your guy which speeds and pressures feel the most pleasurable to him.

SECRET

DON'T NEGLECT THE TIP

The head of an erect penis is like a sensual switchboard, lit up with more nerve endings than any other part of his genitals. Remember the frenulum (that tiny piece of flesh on the underside of the tip, where the head meets the shaft)? "Many men feel the most intense sensations when

3 Sex Myths Busted

There is a lot of misinformation out there about what gets guys off between the sheets. Well, it's time to set the record straight.

MYTH 1

Men think manual action is a total bore.

Fact

Most men love hand jobs. After all, when you think about it, it's how they give themselves pleasure. What men don't love are bad hand jobs. To perfect your manual MO, take your cue from the master, i.e., your guy. The best way to learn how to give a good hand job is to watch him masturbate, since he's ultimately the real expert on his own body.

But if he's a little shy about giving you a do-it-himself demonstration, here's a manhandling move that can't miss: Stand behind him and reach around to his front to pleasure him. It mimics the angle he uses when he's on his own.

MYTH 2

He doesn't want your teeth near his member.

Fact

While no guy wants you gnawing on him, most find receiving little love nibbles pretty fantastic. The problem with using your chompers only arises when they scratch his skin or you accidentally bite down too hard. His testicles are also prime territory for some light dental work, but make sure you tread with extreme caution: It's enough to simply hold a testicle in your mouth (gently, of course) without actually biting down on it.

The only spot that should always remain a totally teeth-free zone is the frenulum, the thin, nerve-centric piece of skin that runs along the underside of a man's penis.

MYTH 3

If you get a little kinky, he'll think less of you.

Fact

The madonna/whore complex is more dated than dial-up computer modems. Seriously, any quasi-evolved man who's worth your time knows full well that a woman who's willing to push the bedroom boundaries a little bit (or, heck, even a lot) is worth more than box seats at the Super Bowl for him and all of his buddies.

So go ahead—play dress up, gently bind his hands behind his head, and smack his cute-as-hell behind hard enough to deliver a pleasurable sting. There's little doubt that he'll find your bad-girl efforts incredibly exciting.

this area is directly stimulated," explains Laurence Levine, MD. Bring him bliss by holding the base of his penis firmly with one hand, then delicately flicking his frenulum with the flat of your tongue. "Use a steady pulsing motion, so you're almost fluttering your tongue against him," says New York City sexuality educator Logan Levkoff. Take breaks by swirling your tongue around his crown or brushing your lips against the tip before returning to his frenulum.

3 SECRET
MIX UP YOUR TOUCH

If any one area of the body—including the frenulum—gets too much stimulation at one time, it becomes desensitized or painful (think of how you feel when your clitoris is over-

TINGLE TRICKS

Send shivers down his spine during your next sack session.

Add Fizzle

Take a swig of peppermint schnapps, crème de menthe, or champagne during sex, then run your tongue along your man's lips and neck—bonus points for sucking the nerve-packed slope between his outside lower lip and chin. "Alcohol contains acid, which adds a tingle, and it evaporates quickly, leaving behind an invigorating, skin-tensing sensation," says Carol Queen, PhD, staff sexologist at goodvibes.com.

Get Fresh

To create thrilling chills during oral action, pop a mint, cough drop, or pea-size amount of toothpaste in your mouth first. Then take your torturous time kissing down your guy's torso—along the sensitive ridges of his abs and up his often-ignored inner thighs—before finally moving his member into your mouth.

Spice Up Sex

Experience a peppery total-body tingle with a cinnamon-flavored lubricant that heats up on contact. Start with an allover sensual massage, rubbing some of the oil on him with your breasts instead of your fingers.

Barely Touch His Body

Run your fingertips, lips or, better yet, a feather down your guy's back for a literally spine-tingling effect.

Freeze Your Foreplay

Skin responds to the slightest temperature changes, so make ice out of fizzy seltzer, then rub him down with the bubbly cubes or blow ice shavings along his bod. Follow that by breathing warm air onto the wet parts—heat increases circulation, making skin even *more* sensitive.

worked—not good). Mixing up your manual moves between two different spots on his body is a good way you can avoid over-stimulating any one region.

Try this technique—think of it as a mock ménage à trois. Ask your guy to close his eyes, then keep one of your hands either

SECRET 4

TREAT HIS JEWELS GINGERLY

His testicles have their own nerve system, developed for protection. That makes them particularly sensitive to changes in temperature and pressure. You can exploit that physiological fact

sible. (Use the same barely-there pressure you use when you move your computer mouse.) "The whole key here is enhanced arousal, and sometimes a little exploration can yield very exciting results," says Dr. Levine.

All that varied hand action will make him feel like he's with two women at once— like a mock ménage à trois.

around his penis or touching his testicles, and use the other hand to scratch his inner thighs or stroke his butt. All that varied hand action will make him feel like he's with two women at once, which is a fantasy that most—okay, all—men have at some point in time.

to bring him more bliss during a hand job or oral sex. But wait until he's already charged up before gently incorporating them into your play. While performing oral sex, cup both twins in the palm of your free hand. Then lightly squeeze them—in tempo with your mouth moves, if pos-

SECRET 5

LET HIM PUT HIS HANDS ALL OVER YOU

It's infinitely more exciting for a man to be touched if he's exploring your bod simultaneously, says Howard J. Ruppel Jr., PhD, chancellor of the Institute for Advanced Study of Human Sexuality. Guys love to be active in the sack—so let him run his hands over your breasts or your butt while you work on him: It will bring him that much more satisfaction. ■

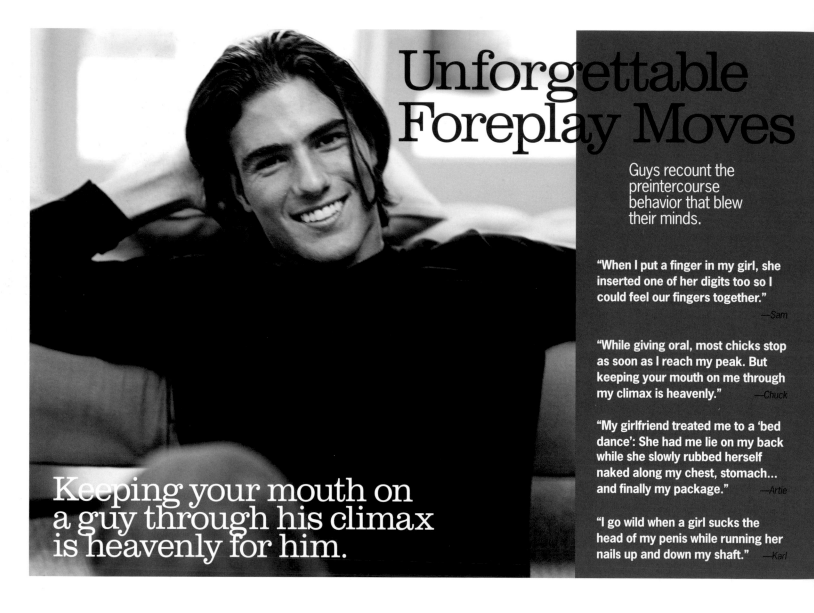

Unforgettable Foreplay Moves

Guys recount the preintercourse behavior that blew their minds.

"When I put a finger in my girl, she inserted one of her digits too so I could feel our fingers together."
—Sam

"While giving oral, most chicks stop as soon as I reach my peak. But keeping your mouth on me through my climax is heavenly."
—Chuck

"My girlfriend treated me to a 'bed dance': She had me lie on my back while she slowly rubbed herself naked along my chest, stomach... and finally my package."
—Artie

"I go wild when a girl sucks the head of my penis while running her nails up and down my shaft."
—Karl

Keeping your mouth on a guy through his climax is heavenly for him.

"Squirt lotion on your butt and let me rub my penis between your cheeks." —Mitch

"One time, my girl got all feisty and pretended not to want to kiss me. I had to use my tongue passionately to pry her mouth open." —Ron

"Sometimes my girl tweaks her nipples between her fingers. They get hard right before my eyes." —Nicholas

"Do what my last girlfriend did: Moan my name over and over again while I pleasure you." —Eddie

"It's so hot when a girl curls her legs tightly around mine as we kiss deeply. It makes me feel like she wants me so bad that she can barely restrain herself from scaling me like a tree." —Willis

"Reach your hand into your panties, then touch my lips with your wetness." —Troy

"Giving me oral is always good, but using your hand as an extension of your mouth is way better and will always leave me weak in the knees." —Peter

"I love the way my girl gives me oral: I kneel at the head of the mattress with my back to the wall. She spreads out stomach-down the length of the bed, so I have a view of her hot body." —Clay

"Lick my fingers and then lead them down into your panties." —Bob

"Dangle your hair between my legs and shake your head. I get chills everywhere." —Kyle

"Position the lights so I can see our shadows on the wall. When you're giving me oral sex, I get turned on by seeing the silhouettes." —Chris

"Rub my penis against your lips, like you're applying lipstick." —Henry

"During a hand job, move my penis all around like an old-school video-game joystick—up, down, side to side, in a circle." —Spencer

"I'm a boob man, so when my girlfriend grazes her nipples against my chest, I feel this tingle shoot between my legs on the way to getting rock hard." —Tony

How to Teach a Guy to Please You

▶ Now that you know all about making your guy happy in the sack, it's time to clue him in to *your* carnal needs. After all, the way he enjoys being touched is probably way different from the way you like it. That's why it's up to you to communicate your between-the-sheets desires. And though it may feel a little awkward to direct a lover, especially a new one, trust us: He wants to know exactly how to satisfy you.

He'll delight in peeling back your petals.

Learn to Be Heard in Bed

In order to have mind-blowing sex, you need to be able to vocalize what you want…or at least give a guy a nudge in the right direction. Communication is an essential ingredient of great sex, but granted, expressing your innermost desires isn't always easy.

There are good ways to spur him into action (such as gently moving his hand to the spot where you want to be caressed or asking him to touch you there) and bad ways (such as forcefully repositioning his hand or barking commands at him like a drill sergeant). The key to talking about sex so you end up with positive results is to ask for what you want without commenting on performance—so speak in terms of enjoyment or preference instead of finding fault.

And while we're on the topic of communication, sexual honesty is essential to achieving real intimacy and pleasure. If you've been faking orgasms, you owe it to yourself (and to him) to stop. If you've faked it only a few times, you don't have to disclose your deception, but you have to start demonstrating what you do like. For example, say, "The way you're touching me feels so good. Now if you could move up just a tiny bit and touch me…right there."

If you feel too shy to say the words, you still have an option. Indicate to him that he's struck gold by letting out a gratified sigh when he's doing something you really, really like.

If you try this subtle trick and you're still not having pleasurable experiences, you're going to have to muster up the guts to be straightforward. Some helpful hints: Don't broach the topic immediately after sex or he may feel like you're criticizing his style or, worse his skills. Instead, find a mellow moment, such as in bed before foreplay or while cuddling together on the sofa, to tell him that you want to strive for an even better sex life with him and offer some solutions.

Be forthcoming but brief, and then suggest what you think you need—different sex positions, for example, or more foreplay—in the most seductive terms you can imagine. Most men will be completely receptive.

Men focus mainly on their erection as a gauge of their excitement level. As a result, they often don't realize how much touching you need to get truly aroused. So encourage your guy to lavish some attention on your nongenital erogenous zones before he dives below your belt.

Lou Paget suggests nudging him to give you the Swirl. "Have him use his fingertips to trace slow, soft circles and waves along your forearms, neck, the palms of your hands, and any other sensitive body part," says Paget. "The irregular motion of circular, wavy touch electrifies the nerves under your skin more than if he just ran his fingers up and down in a straight line."

Experiment with different speeds and directions. One amazing sensation: Have him trace circles on your breasts—

gradually getting closer and closer to your nipples. Or ask him to make incredibly tiny, circular motions using just one fingertip on your clitoris.

Another thing many women find pleasurable is the combination of their partner's hands and mouth on them at the same time, says Laura Berman, PhD. If you're too self-conscious to ask outright for a certain kind of attention, try this sexy tactic: Put his forefinger in your mouth and

suck on it, mimicking the exact motion you'd like him to use on you with your tongue. Paget offers this script for what to tell him beforehand: "This is what I want you to do between my legs—and it would be incredible if you touched me with your fingertips at the same time."

Make sure you praise him (a lot!) when he does something right. That's probably the single most important aspect of getting what you want in bed. Phrases

like "I love that," "Oh, my God!" and the clear, concise "Yes, yes, yes!" work well because they let a guy know without question that he's turning you on. Once he realizes he's rocking your world, he won't want to stop—and he'll remember those winning moves in the future. Another surefire way to get him to please you silly? Show him the special "Show This to Your Guy!" chapter on the following page. ■

One thing many women find pleasurable is the feel of their partner's hands and mouth on them at the same time.

Foreplay-for-Her Rules Every Man Should Follow

1 Slooow Down

On average, it takes a woman roughly 10 to 20 minutes to become completely aroused. Start by telling her how sexy she is (women never get sick of hearing that) and how good you want to make her feel.

Follow this make-her-moan map: Starting at her neck, teasingly graze her skin with your lips, like you were going to kiss her but changed your mind at the last second. Then double back and nip and suck on her earlobe. Stand behind her and run your fingers up and down her arms. Hold her hair to one side and kiss all along her shoulders. Massage those tense muscles at the base of her neck, then move to the front to stroke her breasts. With your mouth slightly open so she can feel the heat of your breath, run your lips over her breasts, inner thighs, pelvis, and the curve above her hip.

2 Give Her a Hand

The clitoris plays a vital role in a woman's arousal and, eventually, her orgasm. But she has a lot of other territory that will respond to your touch. Running your hands over her more sensitive areas will help you figure out what moves she responds to. When she shivers or sighs or leans into your touch, you know you've hit a hot spot!

Some suggestions: Trace your fingertips around the edges of her panties. Gently massage her upper inner thighs. Lightly scratch from her outer thighs to the backs of her calves. We know it's tempting to go for the pot of gold between her legs, but here's a tip: What you *don't* touch is just as important as what you do touch—the tease is what drives women wild.

Finally, when she's noticeably steamed up (her bod, writhing before you, is a hint), lightly stroke her clitoris. (Note: The clitoris has more nerve endings than the penis, and they're concentrated in this one tiny area, so it's supersensitive.) With your index, middle, and ring fingers together (remember the Boy Scout salute?), press the flat part of your fingers—not the tips—into her and rub her like you'd massage a tender, sore muscle—gently but firmly in a circle. If you're not sure about pressure level, err on the side of too-soft touching. If she presses against you or seems anxious for more, increase your pressure.

3 Provide Lip Service

With all due respect to your penis, your tongue can provide a unique (and ecstasy-producing) sensation to a woman's vagina. When you're taking off her underwear, go through the layers, touching and licking over her panties, dampening them with your hot breath and then inching them off.

When you're ready to make contact with her flesh, forget about patenting some complicated tongue twister. That's one of the biggest mistakes a guy can make. It sounds silly, but a good, basic oral sex technique is tracing a figure eight with your tongue. The reason it works: Instead of hitting the same spots repeatedly, you stimulate the whole area.

To get a feel for the other things she likes, flick your tongue lightly around the sides and top of her vulva and work your way in toward her clitoris. Draw circles around it with the tip of your tongue. Kiss her there the same way you would her mouth and she'll see stars.

EROTIC ANALOGIES

To get her really hot and bothered, visualize these moves while you work your magic on her.

WHEN YOU'RE:
Touching her inner thighs

PRETEND YOU'RE:
Working clay (c'mon, we know you've seen the movie *Ghost*). It gets blood pumping through that region, priming her for sex.

WHEN YOU'RE:
Nipping at the base of her neck

PRETEND YOU'RE:
Lightly taking sesame seeds off a bun with your teeth

WHEN YOU'RE:
Slipping off her clothes and underwear

PRETEND YOU'RE:
Peeling fruit. Slowly go through the layers.

WHEN YOU'RE:
Going south of her border

PRETEND YOU'RE:
Licking a stamp, only *muuuch* slower

MAKE NOISE
Some women like to hear sighs from the man giving them oral sex. It shows that he's super turned on by the act.

Buzzy Bed Play

▶ It used to be that vibrators were just for unattached chicks jonesin' for their fair share of climaxes. Not anymore. Sixty percent of unmarried women in relationships have used a vibrator, and almost half of those women have used them alone and with their man, according to a study by Laura Berman, PhD.

As a result, there's been a revolution in bed toys that hum—they now come in a range of discreet shapes and sizes. And since it no longer has to feel like you're bringing a second penis into bed, couples are now more open to incorporating vibrators into their sex play. Another bonus: Vibrators increase sexual responsiveness in most females, so using them fuels women's sexual cravings.

Soon you'll be feeling the good vibrations too!

SEX-TOY SHOPPING

Bullet (or Love Egg)
Intended to tickle your clitoral region, this small, battery-powered vibe looks just like its name indicates.

Finger Vibe
The "splint" slides onto a pointer or middle finger, turning his digit into an actual toy. Use it on him as well.

The Glove
With vibrating pads on each fingertip, this whole-hand hummer covers a much larger surface and can be used to massage your entire body.

Oral Vibe
To add a little something extra to oral action, your man puts this miniature moan-maker on his tongue. A plastic ring keeps the toy in place.

Remote-Control Pantie Vibe
This caters to the voyeur in him and the exhibitionist in you. He can control your stimulation from across the room by just pushing a button.

SOURCE: SADIE ALLISON, DHS, AUTHOR OF *TOYGASMS!: THE INSIDER'S GUIDE TO SEX TOYS AND TECHNIQUES*

We've already established that, in general, women need more presex pampering than men. ("It takes the average man 7 minutes to reach orgasm and the average woman 10 to 20 minutes," says Berman.) With the help of a vibrator, you can hit the arousal phase sooner, so you'll be in tandem when you get to intercourse. Plus, using a vibrator involves much less work, so his hand (or tongue) won't go limp from trying to get you into "go" mode.

SOME SCINTILLATING SUGGESTIONS

■ He can use a finger vibe to stimulate you manually or slip an oral vibe on his tongue before going down on you.

■ Chill a finger vibe in the freezer for 30 minutes. Have

Vibrators increase sexual responsiveness in most women, making them crave sex even more.

him glide it over your nipples, stomach, and then gently over your clitoris.

■ You can run a warm bath and drop in lots of bubble bath. While your man is watching, use a waterproof vibrator on yourself, then ask him to take over.

■ Have him rub two vibrating dildos on you simultaneously. Place one in a sensitive spot, like your inner thigh, while the other is on your clitoris. Do the same to him, running one of the vibrators along his scrotum.   ■

"Honey, Meet My Vibrator."

According to a Cosmo poll, **75%** of guys are game for incorporating vibrators into their sex lives. Still, if you're up for testing the waters with a man, you probably shouldn't just whip out a battery-operated bed buddy in the middle of sex.

Mention your desire to try one when you're not in the bedroom so the immediate pressure is off. And since the word *vibrator* may conjure up images of plastic phalluses crossing swords with his own equipment, stick to the less-daunting term *sex toys*.

Explain that since the sex with him is already so amazing, you want to take it to the next level. He'll likely find the idea that you use a vibrator a turn-on, so consider starting by demonstrating how you use one when you're alone.

If you sense that he's worried about a sex toy being a stand-in for him even when he's in the room, opt for a buzzer that's not too intimidating, like the bullet or the finger vibe.

The Art of 69

This intimate position is both daring and delicious.

▶ If you've never tried the highly erotic, mutually satisfying foreplay move called 69, it's high time. Think about it: What could be more sublime than the sensational intimacy of getting and giving oral sex at the same time? It's true that going head to toe requires more coordination and confidence than your average sex move, but the extra effort is definitely worth it.

Before you get started, you may want to suggest taking a shower together—it's a great way to set the mood and ease your mind about allowing such a close-up view of yourself or any intimate odors.

Certified sexologist Kenneth Ray Stubbs, PhD, author of *Kiss of Desire*, suggests some sexy 69-position variations.

3 Pleasing Positions

SIDE BY SIDE

Slide your body so your head is pointing toward his feet. As you start sucking, bend your top leg back so that your knee is in the air and your foot is flat on the bed. Creating a triangle with your legs invites him to rest his head on your bottom thigh while he works his mouth magic.

YOU ON TOP

Straddle his chest facing away from him, and let him guide your

HOT HINT: Rounding your back ever so slightly makes it easier for him to reach you with his mouth.

hips back so that you're in a position to be pleasured. An even hotter way to get into this pose is to have him lie across the width of the bed with his head slightly over the edge. Start kissing his mouth upside down, then stand on the floor above him with your knees on either side of his head. Seductively crawl over his head onto the bed and continue kissing and licking your way down his chest, stomach, and finally his penis, until your lower body is in the perfect position over his face. Hot hint: Rounding your back slightly makes it easier for him to reach you with his mouth.

HIM ON TOP

Start going down on him while he's sitting back on his heels with his knees bent and you're lying on your stomach, with your elbows supporting your torso. Then take a two-second breather and roll over onto your back and pull him down so that he's on all fours above you, with his head pointing toward your feet. Now both of you are perfectly poised to exchange oral ecstasy. Man-on-top is a tricky angle for mouth movements, but you can more than make up

for those moments when your mouth can't reach him by manually tantalizing his tush and testicles. One more tip…this one is for advanced lovers only: If you trust your guy to tread carefully, you can encourage him to move his pelvis up and down in a way that simulates intercourse…with your mouth.

MAX-IT-OUT MOVES

■ First, get comfy by making sure your bed is smooth—covers under your bod can be an uncomfortable distraction.

■ If you're shorter than he is, place pillows under his head when you're on top so he can reach you better.

■ When your guy is on top, wrap your palms around his penis to help control how fast and deep he goes.

■ Tell him to insert one or two fingers inside you so that he can stroke your G-spot with a come-hither motion.

■ Massage the spot just under his testicles where you can feel the base muscle of his penis—it will set him ablaze.

■ If you're a moaner, let it out when he rubs you the right way even though your mouth is otherwise occupied. It's a signal to him to keep up the speed and pressure that you're enjoying.

■ If he's going too fast, slow the pace at which you're pleasing him. It will silently cue him to do the same.

■ Give your tired mouth a rest and take a break from going down on him. Lightly press your body against his mouth and then gently move your hips back and forth.

■ While he's on top, instead of using your mouth, let him slide his penis between your breasts.

Worth pointing out: Your guy's erection may wax and wane during the act—it's totally normal, so don't worry that he's losing interest in the position. It happens because his thoughts are alternating between what he's doing to you and what's being done to him. ■

If he's going too fast, slow the pace at which you are pleasing him. It will silently cue him to do the same.

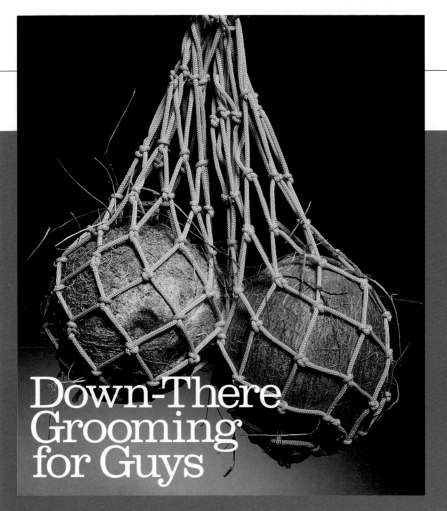

Down-There Grooming for Guys

In this day and age, lots of guys are grooming their pubic hair for all kinds of reasons. For one, they know that less hair on their crown jewels equals a more pleasant oral-sex experience for you—the lack of an overrun, odor-trapping forest makes the whole area more appealing and inviting (how thoughtful). Many men have also noticed that a hairless package is more sensitive. And last but certainly not least is the matter of instant-growth illusion—trimming the hair at the base of the penis can make it look as much as 1 inch longer.

But there may come a day where you run into a guy who isn't as meticulous about his manscaping as you'd like. So why not offer to do the grooming for him...and make it a sexy experience, while you're at it. Some trimming tips:

● Use a blunt-nose pair of scissors, a basic double-blade razor, and perhaps a beard trimmer.

● Have him stand in the shower, but don't turn on the water. Instead, have a bowl of warm water close by.

● Use a hypoallergenic, moisturizing, low-foam shaving cream.

● Shave around the base of the penis, first in the direction of hair growth, then in the opposite direction. Use gentle pressure and rinse the razor in the bowl of water each time it gets clogged.

● On the shaft, use long, light strokes going in the direction of hair growth.

● To defuzz his scrotum, gently stretch the skin to make it taut before running the razor across it. Take your time.

SOURCE: SADIE ALLISON, DHS, AUTHOR OF *TICKLE HIS PICKLE*

Sexy Things to Do With Clothes

▶ Typically, you think of clothes as an obstacle to sex. Well, you're about to learn how they can play a much more exciting role. And we're not talking about dressing up like a cheerleader to act out a guy's fantasy (though that would be fine too). Leaving on an article or two of clothing can create a delicious sense of urgency and provide a visual thrill. So before you strip down, check out these tips for getting your wardrobe in on the lusty action.

Unbuttoning *sloowly* will drive a guy extra wild.

1 Give him a long look at you in a bra, panties, and tall boots. The vixenish-sweet combo majorly turns on men.

2 Blindfold him with his tie. Blocking his sight heightens his other senses, and not knowing what your next move is will drive him insane (in a good way).

3 While wearing a slinky, silky camisole, climb on top of him and then slide your body all over his naked skin.

"My girlfriend bought a shirt that fastened with lots of little hooks. She undid them one by one in a slow striptease."

4 Unzip his pants, but don't pull them off. Instead, insert your hand, gently take his member out of the opening in his boxers, and treat him to some amazing oral action. Trust us, it'll give him a rush to have only this one sexy part exposed.

5 Fling open a front-closure bra right before climax. Setting your breasts free at this pivotal point will send him tumbling over the edge.

6 Whip off his belt, fold it in half, and give his butt a few playful whacks.

7 Gently bind his ankles together using your bra. When you restrict his movement, you get to be in control and he feels the thrill of being dominated by you.

8 Have him place his hands or mouth down south while you're still in your undies The fabric is a barrier (amping excitement), and his warm breath will feel amazing.

9 Sit on top of him, both of you wearing just undies. Grind back and forth against him for as long as you can, then strip and have sex.

10 Just push your underwear aside to have sex. Again, the immediacy of it is hot—like you can't wait to have each other.

11 Don't let him remove his tee shirt before sex. Then, at some pivotal moment— say, midorgasm—grab the fabric in the middle of his chest, twist it so it tightens around his torso, and pull him close.

12 *Slooowly* slip off your panties but keep your skirt on before straddling him for girl-on-top sex. It sends the message that you can't wait a moment longer to have him inside you. ■

SOURCES: GEORGIA CLINICAL SEX THERAPIST GLORIA G. BRAME, PHD; BARBARA KEESLING, PHD, AUTHOR OF *THE GOOD GIRL'S GUIDE TO BAD GIRL SEX*

Cliché as it sounds, men love having sex with a woman who's wearing high heels…and nothing else.

Wanton Wardrobe Tricks

Men talk about the hottest ways women can use clothes to push them over the edge.

"While we're hanging around the house, let part of your bra or panties 'accidentally' peek out. I'll take care of the rest." —Pat

"Strip down naked except for a long string of beads. I adore watching how they roll across your nipples and the rough feel when they get squashed between us." —Brian

"My ex would save old trash-bound lingerie—fishnets, panties, bras—and let me rip them off her during foreplay." —Paul

"Before my girl and I got together, she'd find ways to let me know that

"Feel like getting it on? Walk up to me and stuff a wadded-up pair of panties in my hand. If they're wet, even better. Either way, I know you're not wearing them." —Ted

"When I'm about to go down on you, pull your underwear to the side to allow me access. It lets me know that you're so hot for me that you can't wait long enough for me to slide them off." —Cole

"Tie me up with your clothes as you strip—your bra binds my wrists; your garter belt, an ankle; and so on, and so on...." —Steven

"My last girlfriend liked to take off all of her clothes in front of me—except for her bra and panties. Then she would ask me to carry her over to the bed. Seeing her like that—almost naked and vulnerable—always made me feel like a superhero." —Ben

"Leave some clothes on during sex. The feel of your bra or panties on my skin while we're going at it is incredible." —Matt

she was wearing a garter belt under her skirt—like running down the stairs really fast. Those sexy straps compelled me to get to know her better." —Jeff

"Keep your bra on during doggie-style so I can hold on to the back of it to control some thrusting." —Francisco

"Your guy will always want to go shopping with you if you let him into the dressing room as you try on your clothes—especially lingerie." —Edward

"A miniskirt is the simplest way to turn me on. Seeing you show off your legs makes my mind wander to other parts of your body." —Mark

"I was seeing this girl and her air conditioning broke, so she pranced around in her bikini. It only stayed on for five minutes before I untied the strings with my teeth." —Kyle

"Wear an easy-access skirt when we're out for dinner. Then whisper that you want to have 'dessert' in the bathroom." —Hank

YOUR
SEX
CYCLE

DAY 12

DAY 20

Your Secret Sex Cycle

▶ Ever notice how some days, you're climbing the walls for sex, and others, a frozen yogurt seems more enticing than hopping into bed? Well, blame it on biology. While men have a steady stream of hormones coursing through their bods every day, most women's bodies follow a distinct 28-day sex cycle. "Your cycle marks the rise and fall of your hormones during one month as you move toward or away from ovulation," explains ob-gyn Lisa Masterson.

And by understanding your libido's peaks and valleys, you can pinpoint the days when you're feeling especially aroused and primed for intense pleasure. How cool is that?

HIS
SEX
CYCLE

Days 1 to 11

SLOWLY REVVING UP

When your period kicks off, your sex hormones are lying low, but that doesn't mean your libido is. While some chicks are squeamish about having "period" sex, others are up for action. "The drop in hormones during menstruation relieves PMS symptoms, which puts some women in the mood for sex because they feel more even-keeled," explains Dr. Masterson.

However, from days 6 to 11 after your period is over, you may not feel as horny because your hormones are directed toward building the lining of your uterus and prepping your body for pregnancy.

PASSION POINTER If you want to have sex but are having trouble generating lusty energy,

take a few minutes before drifting off to sleep or while lathering up in your morning shower to fantasize about you and your man really getting it on. "Consciously devoting time to fantasizing about sex can help build arousal when you're going through a lull," says Laura Berman, PhD.

carnal combo of estrogen and testosterone) are rising. Around days 14 to 16, you ovulate (meaning your body releases an egg to be fertilized), which is followed by an increase in progesterone, and you're likely more ravenous for sex. It's nature's way of getting you primed for nooky because you're at your

son. In fact, a study conducted by Newcastle University, in England, found that women are considered better-looking by both sexes during these high-fertility days.

PASSION POINTER Take advantage of your lustiest peak by grabbing your guy for a quickie before work. And if you're solo, indulge in some self-love. "You're experiencing heightened arousal, so any kind of sexual activity will feel more intense," explains Bat Sheva Marcus, clinical director of the Medical Center for Female Sexuality in Purchase, New York.

Take advantage of your lustiest peak by grabbing him for a quickie before work.

Days 12 to 16

YOUR HOTTEST GUY-ATTRACTING WINDOW

On day 12, you may want to try friskier positions or jump your man the minute he walks through the door. That's because your hormone levels (a

most fertile (all the more reason not to forget birth control).

You also happen to be in major man-attracting mode. "Estrogen can help clear up your skin and makes your breasts fuller, which, from a reproductive standpoint, draws a mate to you," notes Dr. Master-

Days 17 to 28

A SECOND PASSION PUSH

Around day 17, your libido starts to lag. Your estrogen level drops, but the progesterone level keeps on climbing,

111

so if you're not pregnant, PMS symptoms may start to creep in around day 22 or 23. Some women experience a second burst of lust around day 20, possibly because of the spike in progesterone. By day 25, your progesterone level takes a nosedive. Shortly after, you start your period and the whole cycle begins all over again.

PASSION POINTER If you're lucky enough to get that sexual second wind, make the most of it with some marathon mattress sessions. If PMS has deflated your desire, keep in mind that orgasms can help relieve cramps. "Ask your partner to give you a full-body massage or try masturbating," suggests Berman. "You don't have to go all out." ∎

Are You on the Pill?

These help free your mind...so your bod can follow.

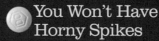

If you're taking birth-control pills, your body doesn't follow the same schedule as non–Pill users. "The Pill creates an artificial cycle by sending a regular dose of hormones into your body each day, which blocks ovulation," explains Lisa Masterson, MD. "These hormones help you stay even-keeled emotionally throughout the month." As a result, you don't experience the same hormonal highs and lows as women who aren't taking the Pill. Here, three key things to know about your Pill-driven cycle:

ⓐ You Won't Have Horny Spikes

Sadly, you won't get that burst of lust that you'd normally have during the few days before and after ovulation, but that doesn't mean you're never going to get turned on. "The Pill allows women to have sex without worrying about getting pregnant, which can make the experience more enjoyable, and that in turn can increase their overall desire for sex," says Leslie Miller, MD, clinical associate professor of obstetrics and gynecology at the University of Washington, in Seattle.

Your Body May Go Through Changes

Some women who take estrogen-heavy pills experience an increase in breast tenderness and even clearer skin, while those who take progesterone-heavy ones may gain weight and experience spotting. The same could also happen with other types of hormone-fueled contraceptives, like the Patch and Nuva Ring. "Try a trial-and-error process with a few different kinds of pills to find the one that suits you best," suggests Dr. Masterson.

Your Libido May Take a Hit

Some Pill takers find the medication sinks their libido and makes it harder to climax.

Though long thought to be psychological, some experts are acknowledging a link between

lower libido and taking the Pill. One theory why: The Pill affects the body's ability to synthesize testosterone—the hormone that helps fuel the sex drive in both men and women.

If your sex drive takes a nose-dive, call your gyno to see if switching to another type of pill reverses the effect. Give your body three months to adjust to the new pill before deciding that it's not working.

On the flip side, if the Pill doesn't impact your sex drive, you may end up having more days when you

feel in the mood than your naturally cycling sisters. Why? Chicks who aren't on the Pill usually endure a week when they're not in the mood for booty (caused by a drop in hormones), but your sex drive can stay the course. "A woman's libido is also heavily influenced by her emotions, and if she's not in the mood for sex, it can be difficult for her to become aroused," adds Dr. Miller.

But women who are on the Pill don't experience this hormonal fluctuation, meaning they may have more days of the month when they may feel sexual.

You Know the Rule– Safety First

▶ Yes, you're a big girl and smart enough to know how important it is to have safe sex without us harping on it. That said, it would be remiss to write this all-encompassing erotic tome and not say a word or two about protecting yourself, especially given how easy it is to slip up.

You've probably been there—so out-of-your-mind-excited in the heat of the moment that you threw caution to the wind and skipped that step where he puts on a condom. Or perhaps you two were buzzed from a night of partying and forgot to use protection. Or maybe

115

he bitched and moaned so much about how "he can't feel anything" when he wears a rubber that you relented and let him go in bareback. Whatever the reason—um, make that excuse—you likely felt guilt-ridden in the morning (or at least you should have).

Well, you really can't afford to mess up again. Now here's where we resort to evil scare tactics: According to the Centers for Disease Control and Prevention, there are an estimated 19 million new sexually transmitted disease infections each year. And STDs—such as the silent, fertility-wrecking chlamydia—are on the rise, with an approximately 2.8 million cases per year. Then of course there is human papillomavirus, or HPV (50 percent of sexually active men and women acquire

CONDOM SHOPPING

MATERIALS

Latex (a type of rubber)

PROS The safest, most readily available, and least expensive

CONS Up to 6 percent of the population is allergic to latex, according to the American Academy of Allergy, Asthma, and Immunology.

Polyurethane (a type of plastic)

PROS Plastic is thinner and less constricting than latex.

CONS They're not as widely available. Studies have found that they break and slip more often than latex does.

WARNING: Condoms made from lambskin don't protect against STDs.

HOT SHAPES AND STYLES

Textured (Ribbed, nubbed, studded) They supply added texture, which stimulates nerve endings in the vaginal wall. (However, some women say they can't feel a difference.)

Pouched Pouched condoms have "pockets" on the sides or near the tip. They're designed to be looser fitting in the areas that cover the penis, increasing friction and sensitivity for him.

Ultrathin The thinner the latex, the more sensation you'll both feel. There's no evidence to suggest these thinner condoms are any more likely to break if used as directed.

Colored/Flavored/Glow-in-the-Dark
These condoms are a great way to add playfulness and ease some of the tension, which ultimately leads to hotter sex.

WARNING: Any condom labeled "for novelty use only" is not FDA approved and does not offer protection of any kind.

SOURCE: ADAM GLICKMAN, CEO OF CONDOMANIA.COM

HOW TO GET A GUY TO ACTUALLY WEAR ONE

it and it can lead to cervical cancer in women), and human immunodeficiency virus, or HIV, which is potentially fatal.

Hearing those facts is very frightening (not to mention a total buzz kill), but knowing the truth should motivate you to take complete control of your sexual health.

Here's what you've gotta do: When having sex outside a totally monogamous relationship in which you've both been tested for sexually transmitted diseases, you need to protect yourself each and every time you have a roll in the hay (or a roll in those 400-thread-count sheets you blew the bank on). And the absolute best way to protect yourself is with a condom. Stop cringing! We're Cosmo—and we've found a way to make even STD prevention sexy and fun. Besides, to have really satisfying sex, you have to be relaxed. And that means not stressing out over having irresponsible sex. ■

In a perfect world, the guy you're sleeping with would've already gone to the store to buy condoms without your even asking. But the truth is, many men require a little prodding, if not a full-on shove out the door. A recent study by the Kinsey Institute found that 28 percent of men reported losing an erection while putting on a condom one of the last three times they had sex.

That's why when asking a guy to wear a condom, "you need to be direct but also mention what's in it for him," says sex therapist Louanne Cole Weston, PhD. "Tell him you want to be less inhibited, which requires being protected."

117

THE HOTTEST WAYS TO PUT ONE ON

With the right moves, you can make the roll-on a sizzling foreplay maneuver. First, make sure the reservoir tip is facing up so you don't put on the condom inside out (if you accidentally do, throw the condom away and use a new one). Then start by gently pinching about half an inch at the top and unrolling the condom down to the base of his shaft, smoothing out any air bubbles as you go along.

"Keep massaging his testicles after the condom is on," says sex therapist Ian Kerner, PhD. You can also add a few drops of lube and give him a couple of strokes that will take his mind off the fact that he's wearing a rubber.

If you're really out to impress, consider rolling the condom on him with your mouth (it's easier than it sounds). Here's how: Lube your lips with a water-based lubricant, purse them as if you're kissing, and use gentle suction to hold the condom (you might want to use a nonlubricated condom or a flavored condom) in your mouth with the reservoir tip pointing toward your throat and the ring of the condom outside your lips. Press the reservoir tip against the roof of your mouth with your tongue to keep the air out of the tip as the condom is going on.

At this point you could put a bit of water-based lubricant on your guy's penis for an added boost of sensitivity. Using one or both of your hands, grasp the base of his shaft to keep it hard and straight. If he's uncircum-

CONDOM TROUBLESHOOTING

One of You Is Allergic to Latex

If reactions such as itching and burning occur, try polyurethane, and avoid condoms with spermicide, especially nonoxynol-9, which can cause irritation even if you aren't allergic.

Condoms Make Him Lose His Erection

In addition to larger or thinner condoms, he can try a cock ring (placed at the base of the shaft and around his testicles), which keeps the blood supply from draining from the penis.

cised, make sure his foreskin is pulled back. Lower your head and put the condom on the tip of his penis.

Make sure you have the reservoir tip squeezed with your tongue against the head of the penis. Wrap your lips over your teeth, and use one smooth motion to roll the condom down the shaft of the penis. Use your index fingers and thumbs to unroll the condom all the way down if you have to. Voilà! Only a really amazing lover can pull that off. ∎

TRICKS MOST GIRLS DON'T KNOW

∎ Try a condom that has a warming agent in the lubricant. The heat provides a new sensation.

∎ Put a drop of water-based lube inside the tip of the condom to increase sensitivity.

∎ Give a vibrating condom ring a whirl. It fits at the base of the penis (over the condom). The tiny buzzing motor is strategically placed to hit your clitoris. ∎

He Ejaculates Too Soon
If your guy is more of an Olympic-level sprinter than a marathon man, try Trojan Extended Pleasure condoms, which are lubricated with a slight numbing agent called benzocaine that may keep him in the race longer.

The Rubber Breaks
Wash yourself with soap and water, and see a doctor ASAP to be tested for STDs. If you're not on birth control and are over 18, you can get emergency contraception over the counter; under 18, a doc can prescribe it. Call 888-NOT-2-LATE.

119

This section is called The Main Event
because that's really what intercourse is,
isn't it—the much-anticipated pinnacle
of a sexual experience? It's when you're
most physically connected with a lover.
And not surprisingly, it's the act that
helps intensify that emotional bond
between you and him.

   In this section we have loads of
advice for making the main event both
mind-blowing and meaningful. You'll
find 21 sizzling sex positions to try,
orgasm-enhancing tips, and suggestions
for places you've never even *thought*
of to do the deed. You'll also learn the
key to taking sex to a deeper, more
intimate level and how to treat the man
in your life to a more thrilling bedroom
experience than he's ever imagined.

event the main event the main event the main eve

We know what you're thinking: "I'll have what she's having, thank you very much."

Orgasms During Intercourse

▶ Let's be real: Having an orgasm through oral or manual stimulation is awesome. Still, most women who have orgasms want to be able to climax during intercourse, although less than 50 percent reveal that they've actually been able to do so, according to the Kinsey Institute for Research in Sex, Gender, and Reproduction at Indiana University in Blooming-ton. Fifty percent doesn't sound like a great statistic, but there's no reason *you* can't be one of the women who do experience intercourse orgasms. (And if every chick got her hands on this book, the number would definitely climb!) It helps to have a few tricks, like the ones we have here.

GET AT THE RIGHT ANGLE

An important little piece of info you may not know: The angle of your legs can make all the difference in your pleasure. "Generally, it's easier for women to orgasm when they keep their knees below their hips," says Felice Dunas, PhD. To do this, put a pillow under your butt or lie on the edge of the bed with your legs dangling off during missionary-style sex.

A pillow or two can help you strike the perfect pose.

These positions increase tension in your groin muscles, which stimulates the nerves in your pelvic region and increases your chances of climaxing," says Dunas.

These positions stimulate nerves in the pelvis, upping your chances of climaxing.

 MAKE CLITORAL CONTACT

By lifting your butt (or lowering your legs), you'll also get his pubic bone rubbing closer to your clitoris. (Remember, your clitoris is there for one reason and one reason only: sexual satisfaction.)

Another lovemaking method that provides plenty of clitoral friction is called the coital alignment technique (CAT). Here's how it's done: Have your man enter you in the missionary position then lift himself up the length of your body about 2 inches so that the base of his penis hits your clitoris. In this "riding high" position, ask him to move in a way that's more up and down than in and out. Keep him close by grabbing on to his tush and pressing him against you. For deeper penetration, try wrapping your legs around his thighs and hooking your ankles around his calves. While he makes a shallow rocking motion, push your pelvis up

NO SNAP JUDGMENTS! The erect length of a penis can't be reliably predicted when in a flaccid state, since men have different degrees of retraction.

and grind your clitoris into him. (It's a good idea to move at the same time as he does.)

The beauty of the CAT is that it gives women the constant clitoral stimulation they need to orgasm during sex. Plus, the guy still gets in enough thrusting action to get off, so it's a win-win situation for everybody. But listen, don't get bummed if making the CAT work for you takes some practice—it's a little tricky! Trust us, it's worth the time and effort.

GIVE YOURSELF A HAND

In the interim, there's an easier way to gain an orgasmic edge:

The cowgirl position is one of his all-time favorites.

Stroke yourself during sex. At first, it might feel like a weird thing to do when there's a man in the room, but think about it this way—guys do whatever it takes to reach orgasm and you should too. What's more, Cosmo sex polls show time and again that guys want to see you touch yourself while you two are doing the deed. I mean—*hello*—it's hot and it takes the pressure off him to ensure you climax.

Still, if you've never done it before, it's natural to feel vulnerable having your man watch you masturbate. One way to ease into it: Try stimulating yourself during doggie-style sex—it might help you relax if your partner isn't looking right at you.

Once you get more comfortable letting your hands wander south in front of your guy, let him get an eyeful of the action. Men,

Men are visual creatures, and few things get them more excited than watching a woman stroke her own body.

as you know, are incredibly visual creatures, and few things get them more excited than watching a woman stroke her own body. Some positions that allow for that: In cowgirl (you sitting on top), slide your hand over your labia, and slowly stroke yourself from your clitoris down along the edges of the lips to the back of your vagina (near the base of his member) and back

SURPRISING ORGASM ROADBLOCKS

HIGHWAY CLOSED AHEAD

1 TUNING OUT
It's hard not to let your mind drift, but if you find yourself making a mental grocery list mid-act, you need to re-engage your body. Try focusing solely on sensations—how he feels inside you and how your body is responding.

2 FORGETTING TO PEE
Since G-spot stimulation can make you feel like you have a full bladder, use the bathroom before sex. That way, when you're about to orgasm, you'll know that you don't have to urinate, and you'll be better able to stay in the moment.

3 CHANGING POSITIONS TOO OFTEN
The key to satisfaction for many women is steady stimulation in a position that hits their pleasure points. Instead of constantly switching around, develop a rhythm, and once you feel yourself building toward climax, stay the course.

up, moving your hand with the rhythm of your thrusts. Or just focus on lightly rubbing your clitoris. "The dual stimulation from your guy's penis and your hand on your clitoris can lead to a very powerful climax," explains Laura Berman, PhD.

Another supersizzling move: While in the missionary position, make a V with your first two fingers and place them around your vagina so that his member slides in and out between them. "You're touching your clitoris, inner labia, and the area surrounding the urethra, which are chock-full of nerve endings," says Berman. "Plus, he'll love the feel of your fingers on his penis." You can also do this while lying on your back with your legs on his shoulders (the angle exposes your clitoris and vagina).

Size Matters

He's Too Small

It can be a letdown when you discover that a guy's penis seems, oh, about 80 times smaller than your ex's. But if you like the guy and have good sexual chemistry with him, there are ways to overcome his, um, shortcomings. First, "a small penis tends to fit nicely against many women's G-spot, whereas a larger one may miss it entirely," says Joy Davidson, PhD, author of *Fearless Sex*.

A good position for hitting that bull's-eye: "Sitting on his lap, facing him, maximizes G-spot pleasure," says relationship therapist Bonnie Eaker Weil, PhD, author of *Make Up, Don't Break Up*, who also offers this trick: "During doggie-style, keep his hips higher than yours, so his penis points toward your vagina's anterior. Also, pulse your PC muscles to create a tighter fit."

And don't forget that your man's hands are pleasure tools too. "If he enhances intercourse with clitoral massage, the size of his member might become a nonissue," says Davidson.

If you have good chemistry, there are ways to deal with his, um, shortcomings.

He's Too Big

It's rare that you hear a woman lament having a well-endowed lover. That's because "the vaginal canal is extremely elastic, and most women can comfortably accept a 5- to 9-inch penis," says sex therapist Judith Seifer, PhD.

However, for the few who do find accommodating a large penis difficult, it's a major obstacle to pleasure. Some advice: Try extending foreplay and delaying penetration until you are fully aroused—the longer you wait, the more lubricated and looser you'll be (the length and width of the vagina increases by as much as 2 inches during excitation). Using a water-based lubricant can also help, as can gently stretching the vagina with your (or your partner's) fingers before entry.

To make sex more comfortable, take the on-top position and guide him in yourself. Doing so will allow you to control how fast and how deep he can go. Last but not least, have sex as much as you can. Explains Seifer: "Think of intercourse as a workout for your vaginal muscles: The more you do it, the better your muscles become at stretching and contracting." And don't worry—you won't be "ruined" for a smaller guy later on.

On the other hand, you can also give your guy a private tutorial in how to turn you on with his own fingers, which he's guaranteed to love.

During girl-on-top sex, take your man's hand and have him circle the area immediately surrounding your clitoris gently with his thumbs. If he's strong enough to support himself on one arm during rear entry, have him reach around with one hand to stimulate your clitoris. (Hot hint: Tell him to wet his fingers first with either saliva or a water-based lubricant.) Reverse cowgirl (the move where you're on top riding him while facing his feet) also allows a man plenty of room for manual manipulation—especially if you recline so that your back is practically resting on his chest.

 ## HIT THE G-SPOT

Another blissful orgasm (which feels completely different) entails stimulating your G-spot. Hopefully you discovered your G-spot's whereabouts during a sexy solo mission. (See the Preplay section of this book.) If not, here's a recap: It's situated halfway between your vaginal opening and your cervix on the front wall of the vagina. If you imagine a small clock inside your vagina with 12 o'clock pointing toward the navel, most women's G-spots are between 11 and 1. It feels like a spongy, dime-size area, though after some stimulation, the spot will become hard (sorta like a penis does) and swell to about the size of a quarter.

Just as you have to experiment with strokes and pressure to have

Reverse cowgirl allows a man plenty of room for manual manipulation, especially if you recline a little.

a clitoral orgasm, you need to condition your G-spot to climax too. So before you have him probe the area with his penis, try these techniques: Use your hand to press the pubic/lower-belly border downward to stimulate the outside of the G-spot while his finger caresses the inside. Or test-drive this amazing maneuver: Have him massage the G-spot from within with a "come here" motion until you're just about to climax, then stop. Shift

129

attention to your clitoris until you almost orgasm that way, then stop again. Now go back to your G-spot. Let yourself go over the edge when you can't hold back anymore. Delaying your climax this way will make it incredibly powerful when you do release.

Once your G-spot has been pushed, don't be surprised if a skim milk–like fluid squirts or

orgasm will feel exactly the same—freakin' incredible.

To target the G-spot during intercourse, try positions that have his penis angled toward your belly button. Since many men's erections slant upward, doggie-style and reverse cowgirl are ideal. To send yourself over the edge, bear down with your PC muscles. Not only does this

your arms and push your hips upward. Or try lying on your stomach while he gently lies on top of you so he can penetrate you deeply from behind.

REACH FOR THE BLENDED BIG O

Once you're familiar with clitoral and G-spot orgasms, you can intensify your grand finale by going for a blended orgasm, where you or your partner stimulates your clitoris and your G-spot at the same time.

To send yourself spilling gloriously over the edge, bear down with your PC muscles—remember those?

drips out of your urethra. According to Beverly Whipple, PhD, coauthor of the classic book *The G-Spot*, many women actually ejaculate when they orgasm this way. But don't worry if you don't; either way is perfectly normal and your G-spot

collapse the vaginal walls surrounding the penis for a snugger fit, it also lowers your G-spot so it rubs right up against his penis. More sex positions that facilitate G-spot success? Facing toward him as you straddle his pelvis, especially if you lean back on

One position that allows for this is woman-on-top, in which you angle yourself so that your guy's penis hits your G-spot. Then ask him to massage your clitoris with his thumbs. Once you've reached this pleasure benchmark, there's no going back. ■

Experimentation is
what keeps a couple's
sex life scorching.

21 Sizzling Sex Positions

▶ Most couples have certain go-to positions in their sexual repertoires—passion poses they rely on because they've proved to provide maximum satisfaction. And there's nothing wrong with that.

But at Cosmo, we strongly believe that experimentation is what keeps a couple's sex life sizzling. Over the years, we've pioneered some erotic innovations by putting our own special spin on some classic sex positions. Here, we offer up 10 of our favorite carnal contortions, plus 10 we've created just for this book. Last but not least, we offer up one unbelievably creative bonus position that we're labeling "for advanced lovers." Limber up—and enjoy!

STRADDLE HIS SADDLE

Erotic instructions Have your guy sit on the floor with his arms stretched out behind him for support and his legs crossed loosely Indian-style. Climb onto his lap so you're straddling him in a kneeling position and grip his shoulders as you lower yourself onto his penis. Lean toward him and keep your bodies close together as you control the speed of the thrusting.

Why you'll love it This is the ultimate girl-power position, because you command the action by alternating slow, shallow strokes with deep thrusts. To mix things up a bit, lower yourself down your man's shaft in drive-him-nuts circular motions (like a corkscrew), and this seriously simple sack session becomes one wild ride.

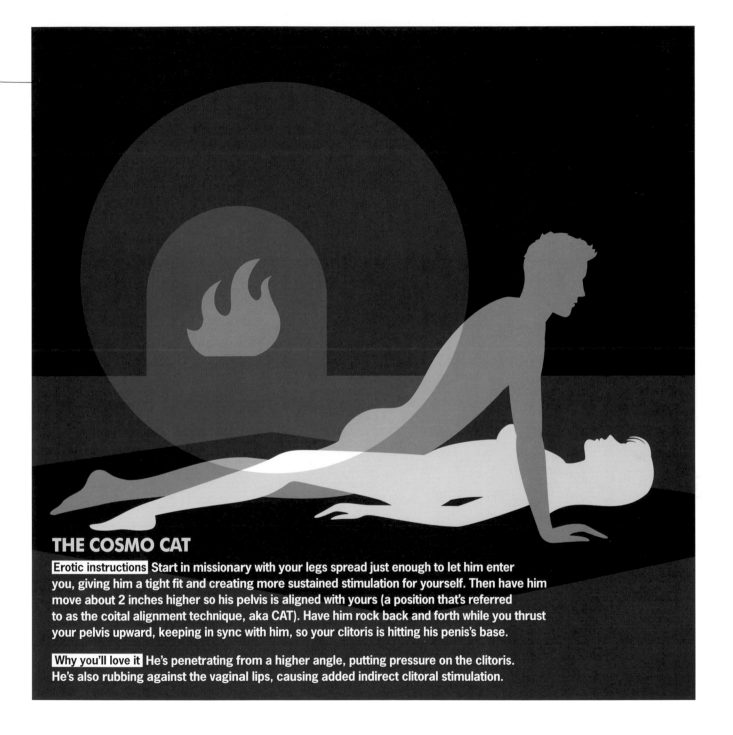

THE COSMO CAT

Erotic instructions Start in missionary with your legs spread just enough to let him enter you, giving him a tight fit and creating more sustained stimulation for yourself. Then have him move about 2 inches higher so his pelvis is aligned with yours (a position that's referred to as the coital alignment technique, aka CAT). Have him rock back and forth while you thrust your pelvis upward, keeping in sync with him, so your clitoris is hitting his penis's base.

Why you'll love it He's penetrating from a higher angle, putting pressure on the clitoris. He's also rubbing against the vaginal lips, causing added indirect clitoral stimulation.

Girl-on-Top Tricks

Year after year, guys tell us that girl-on-top is their absolute favorite sex position. And hey—what's not to like? They get a sexy view of you, it frees up their hands to roam your gorgeous body, and let's face it—you're doing the majority of work. But it's great for women too because it allows you to control the speed and depth of penetration. Check out these little tweaks to make this crowd-pleasing passion pose even better.

- Face your guy and lean back just slightly, your pelvis raised, hands behind you supporting your weight. Then slide up and down his member with slow, steady strokes.

- Have your guy scoot his butt to the edge of the bed and lie all the way back. Lower yourself onto his member while standing on the ground over him. Because you're stimulating different spots on his penis and in your vagina, you'll both feel new sensations.

- Ask him to reach around and knead your behind, simultaneously massaging the fleshiest part of each cheek as you grind.

- Lean forward and firmly suck on his earlobe. To feel that intense sensation suddenly when he's just about to climax will make him lose his mind.

- Face away from him and reach down and cup his testicles as you're thrusting.

- Take your guy's hand and guide him to circle the area immediately surrounding your clitoris (C-spot) gently with his fingers. Get into a slow rhythm so your hands feel in sync. Then slip your digits underneath so his palm is covering your hand while you take over.

- To stimulate your C-spot, arch your body toward him and grind your pleasure point against his pelvis. As you move in and out at this angle, it will stimulate your clitoris. It also creates friction between your vaginal lips, enhancing sensation.

- Grind in circles—not up and down—to prevent slippage. To boost clitoral sensation, rub against his pelvic bone. With these tricks, size won't matter…much.

- Alternate in-and-out thrusts with circular motions.

- Rotate from girl-on-top position into reverse cowgirl (slowly). Not only are you hitting a series of new hot spots for both of you with each different angle, but he'll dig the 360-degree view of your bod.

- Turn around so you're facing away from him. As you thrust, reach down so you can caress his toes or the balls of his feet. The combo is incredibly erotic.

- Don't let him all the way in… at least at first. When you're straddling your guy, lift your hips so that only the head of his penis is penetrating you. Move up and down quickly three times on just the tip. On the fourth count, slide all the way down so he's completely inside you, then go back to teasing just the tip again before you let him reenter you. By not letting him thrust away, you get to hold off his orgasm until you're both ready.

SOURCES: PSYCHOLOGIST MICHAEL BADER, DMH, AUTHOR OF *AROUSAL*; SEX COACH PATTI BRITTON, PHD, AUTHOR OF *THE COMPLETE IDIOT'S GUIDE TO SENSUAL MASSAGE*; PSYCHOLOGIST MICHAEL BRODER, PHD, AUTHOR OF *CAN YOUR RELATIONSHIP BE SAVED?*; AVA CADELL, PHD, AUTHOR OF *STOCK MARKET ORGASM*; SEX THERAPIST JUDY KURIANSKY, PHD, AUTHOR OF *THE COMPLETE IDIOT'S GUIDE TO TANTRIC SEX*

You pick the angle and speed of the thrusting…so it gives you maximum control for an intense orgasm.

BACKUP BOOGIE

Erotic instructions Your partner lies on his back, his legs straight out in front of him, a pillow under his head so he can watch the action. You straddle him with your head facing his feet. With your hands on the floor for support, you back up onto his penis. He holds your upper thighs or butt tightly while you thrust.

Why you'll love it You pick the angle and speed of the thrusting, so there's plenty of opportunity to experiment and find your inside hot spot. Get a rhythm down—circle for a few times before you take an unexpected plunge. It gives you maximum control for an intense orgasm, but your guy gets to savor every sensation without working up much of a sweat. And he'll love the total visual and tactile access to your backside.

THE ROCK & ROLL

Erotic instructions Choose any flat surface—the floor or a even a sturdy table—and lie faceup, bringing your knees as close to your chin as you can. He lies on top of you, and while you rest your calves on his shoulders, your man should enter you just as he would in the missionary position. For some extra leverage, grab hold of his upper arms. He'll likely need to have his palms flat down for support as he begins thrusting inside you. **Why you'll love it** This man-on-top position makes you feel deliciously open and vulnerable, while his incredibly deep thrusting drives you to superorgasmic heights. This is also a good position for extrasensual couples—you're face-to-face, so it's easy for you to make out or nibble on each other's mouths.

HOW TO KEEP HIM "IN" DURING A SWITCH

We've all marveled at Hollywood love scenes where the couple swaps positions with choreographed precision. But in reality, sex isn't always so seamless. People knock heads, get tangled in the sheets, and yes, momentarily disengage. However, if you don't want to stop and reconnect, here's a suggestion: Start in missionary close to the edge of the left side of the bed. Keeping your right leg straight, wrap your left leg around your guy's waist and hook your left arm under his shoulder. Pushing off with your right arm, keep a firm grip on your guy as you roll him onto his back toward the right side of the bed in one motion.

THE HOT SEAT

Erotic instructions Have your partner kneel behind you, but tell him to lean slightly backward. With your back to him, you kneel in front of him, your legs between his. Your bodies should be squeezed together tightly. Wrap his arms around your waist and put your hands wherever you want (his forearms, hips, etc). Once he's inside you, move up and down or swivel your hips in a circular motion in tandem, stopping to take breaks when you get too worked up or tired.

Why you'll love it Since he's tilting back, he has G-spot access. And this position allows for intense pressure since you're meshing your butt super snugly with his groin.

ROMP WITH A VIEW

Erotic instructions Lie on your side on a sturdy surface, with one arm propping up your head or bent under your body for support. Keeping one leg stretched out along the bed or floor, extend the other straight up in the air so it's perpendicular to your body. Your partner can then straddle your grounded leg and enter you while holding your other leg or letting it rest against his shoulder for leverage.

Why you'll love it He can penetrate you in up-and-down motions instead of regular back-and-forth thrusting. The different strokes will bring on new sensations.

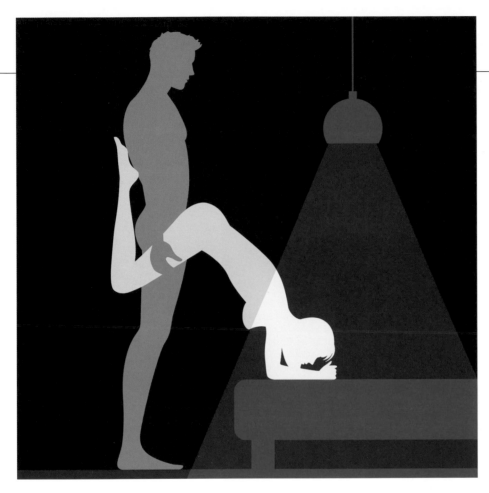

It's a great angle for you and your man will be super turned on by the view he gets of your gorgeous posterior.

UPSIDE DOWN & DIRTY

Erotic instructions Start by standing and facing a bed or a chair. Bend over until your head, upper arms, and elbows are resting on its surface. Have your man stand behind you and grab both of your thighs and raise your legs up so that you're straddling his body. As he enters you from behind, support yourself on the bed by resting on your forearms with your hands clasped in front of you. **Why you'll love it** It's a rockin' alternative for those addicted to the angles and impact of any from-behind ride. Plus your man will be seriously turned on by the bird's-eye view of your posterior. If you get tired, just take periodic rests.

141

TANTALIZING TANGLE

Erotic instructions You and your guy lie on your sides in bed, facing each other. Inch close to his body and scissor your legs as he enters you. While he's thrusting, hold on tight to each other for leverage and to create super-close (and superhot) friction.

Why you'll love it This is a snug-together fit that generates lots of tension yet lets you kiss, nibble, and stroke each other while doing the deed. Plus it's also great for G-spot access—when one leg is up that high, his penis can glide against it. Experiment to find the exact angle that will send you to the moon.

THE OCTOPUS

Erotic instructions Have your guy sit on the floor, legs spread and bent slightly at the knees. Sit between his legs, and raise your legs so your right leg rests on his left shoulder and your left leg on his right shoulder. You will look like a multilimbed lust creature.

Why you'll love it Because your body is tilted upward, your guy enters you using up-and-down motions rather than circular or side-to-side ones, bringing on deep direct G-spot orgasms. And he gets a prime view of all the action—a male fantasy come true!

MOVER & SHAKER

Erotic instructions Lie facedown on top of a washing machine, with your feet flat on the floor (if you're short, try standing on a phone book). Have your guy stand facing your behind, between your legs. Once you're going at it, turn on the machine. Have him lean forward so that his thighs are pressed against you. The vibrations will rock through his entire body.

Why you'll love it The vibrations will feel delicious against your bare body. And every time the machine changes cycles, you'll experience a different sensation. In addition to the shaking, the surface of the washer will create a scintillating heat coming from below. (Just be sure to set the washer on a hot-water cycle.)

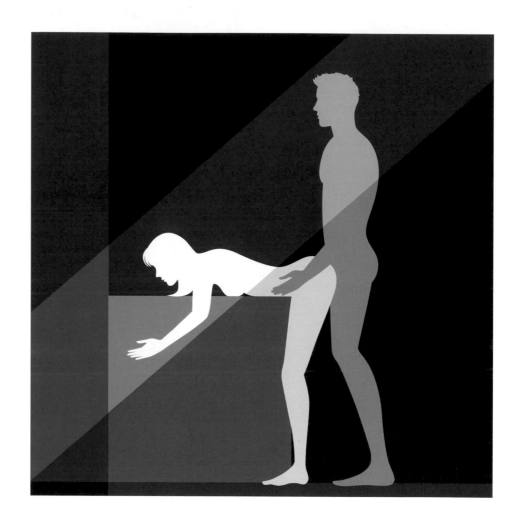

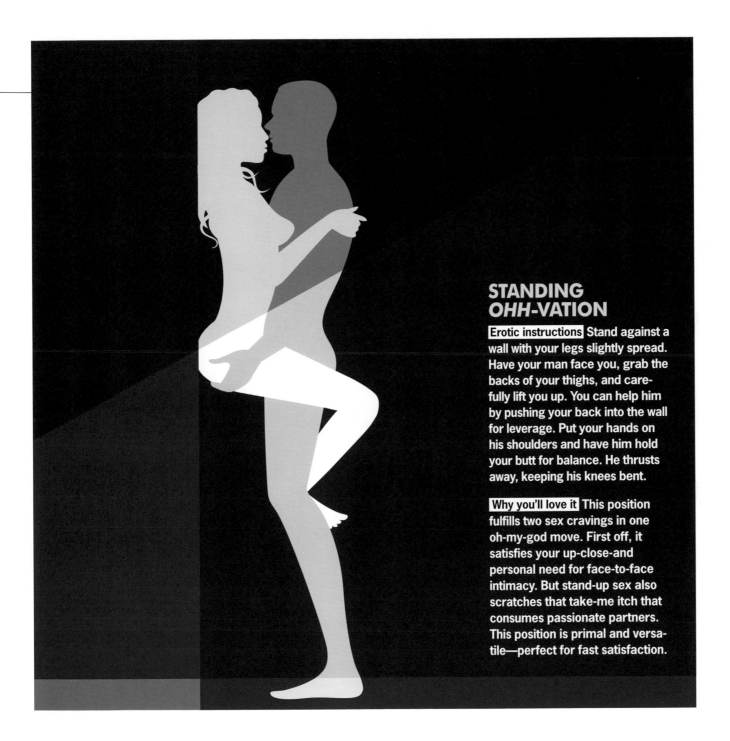

STANDING
OHH-VATION

Erotic instructions Stand against a wall with your legs slightly spread. Have your man face you, grab the backs of your thighs, and carefully lift you up. You can help him by pushing your back into the wall for leverage. Put your hands on his shoulders and have him hold your butt for balance. He thrusts away, keeping his knees bent.

Why you'll love it This position fulfills two sex cravings in one oh-my-god move. First off, it satisfies your up-close-and personal need for face-to-face intimacy. But stand-up sex also scratches that take-me itch that consumes passionate partners. This position is primal and versatile—perfect for fast satisfaction.

Should You Make a Sex Tape?

Pause the passion play and consider this.

Sure, making at-home pornographic flicks can add spice to your sex life. But in this age of digital streaming and instant Web access, women who make the decision to star in a kinky video project don't always come out on top.

Still, making an erotic video or taking sexy pictures can be exciting for some couples, as long as it isn't the mainstay of their sex life, says psychologist I. David Marcus, PhD, of Silicon Valley Psychotherapy Center in San Jose, California. But in some cases, being sexually risqué can be downright *risky*...and not just to your reputation. This kind of experimentation can have repercussions in your relationship. Here are some of the pitfalls.

Overexposure. One of the main risks of making a sex tape is that it could get into the wrong hands. Alarmingly, many guys like to go public with their video masterpiece even when you're still a couple. Amateur sex sites are very popular on the Internet, says Marcus. And when a guy makes a sex tape, a tremendous part of the appeal can be the thrill of posting it publicly and watching himself—and you—online.

Raising the bar too high. According to Mark Schwartz, ScD, clinical codirector of Castlewood Treatment Center in Saint Louis, watching a lot of porn can actually make a man more dependent on similar visual imagery for arousal. "The risk is that men become unable to be stimulated by the human beings beside them," he says. And when this happens, your relationship is on shaky ground.

Second thoughts. One of the cruelest truths of this whole business is that playing around with moviemaking may turn your guy totally off to you in the end. "They may not know it, but some guys don't want to see their girlfriends as porn stars," says Marcus.

D.I.Y. erotica pointers. If you're still hot to press record, follow our rules: First, ask yourself what you want to get out of this blue-movie venture. Then discuss all the dirty details (leave nothing out) with your guy in advance, so you're both on the same page before the camera starts rolling. "You need to anticipate what it will be like in the moment and discuss what will happen if you find you don't enjoy being taped," says Megan Fleming, PhD, a clinical psychologist and certified sex therapist in New York City.

Retain ownership. Protect your privacy by keeping the tapes and JPEGs. Once you put something on tape, it can get out there, warns Marcus. If your guy tries to fight you on this, put your foot down and tell him you're not comfortable doing it otherwise. That said, the safest bet is actually to delete and destroy your home-made documentary immediately after viewing it.

Consider the repercussions. There are external ways to fuel your desire for each other—like making videos and using sex toys—and then there is the emotional spice, which may, in fact, be what your sex life is really missing, says Marcus. In other words, your very own remake of *Debbie Does Dallas* may not be the boundary-pushing exercise your relationship needed.

The stimulation caused by the circular motion will slowly electrify you, bringing on a subtle yet strong orgasm.

SEXY SWIMMERS

Erotic instructions Lie on your stomach, arms raised above your head, legs spread slightly, with a pillow or two placed under your pubic bone. Your partner stretches his body over yours and enters you mimicking the position you're in. He can alternate between from-behind thrusting and a circular, swirling motion.

Why you'll love it The circular stimulation will slowly electrify your vagina, which will bring on a subtle yet superstrong orgasm. There isn't a lot of motion with this position, so it's a good way to delay his peak if he's prone to too-quick climaxing (or if you just want to savor the feel of each other's bodies). If you need more leverage to finish, you can both raise up to your knees.

147

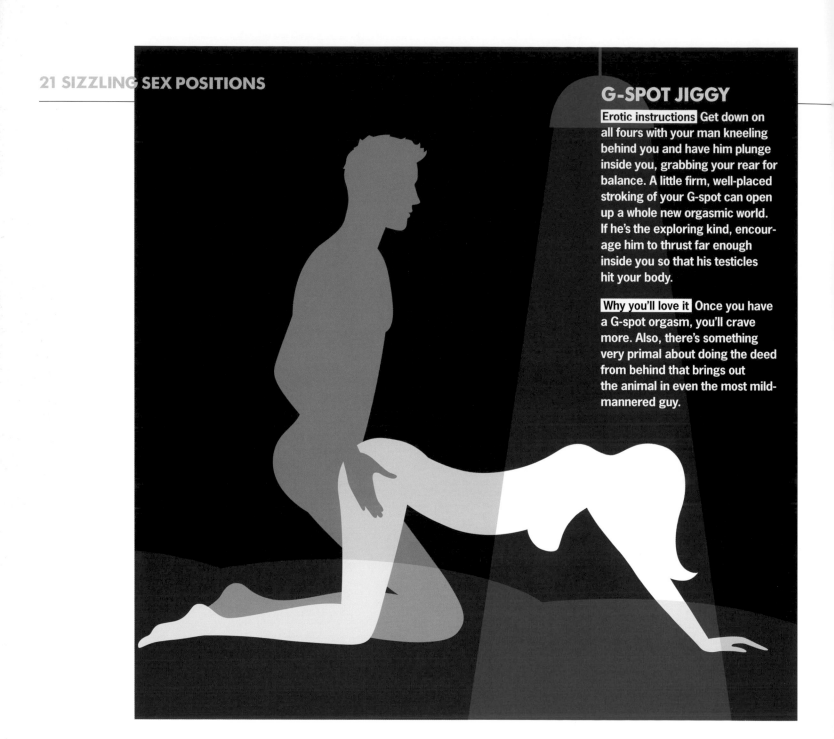

G-SPOT JIGGY

Erotic instructions Get down on all fours with your man kneeling behind you and have him plunge inside you, grabbing your rear for balance. A little firm, well-placed stroking of your G-spot can open up a whole new orgasmic world. If he's the exploring kind, encourage him to thrust far enough inside you so that his testicles hit your body.

Why you'll love it Once you have a G-spot orgasm, you'll crave more. Also, there's something very primal about doing the deed from behind that brings out the animal in even the most mild-mannered guy.

CHEEKY CHALLENGE

Erotic instructions Stand on the edge of a couch, bed, or two chairs, with your legs spread wide. Position your man so he's standing on the floor facing you. Adjust the width of your stance (bending your knees slightly if necessary) so he can easily slide between your legs and get your pelvises to meet. Place his hands on your derriere and yours on his. Then enjoy giving each other butt massages as you rock your bodies together.

Why you'll love it Your stance allows you to move to his rhythm, while your wide-spread legs give you that supersexy, vulnerable feeling. All that frontal friction will hit your hot spot and take you to a no-hands-necessary climax.

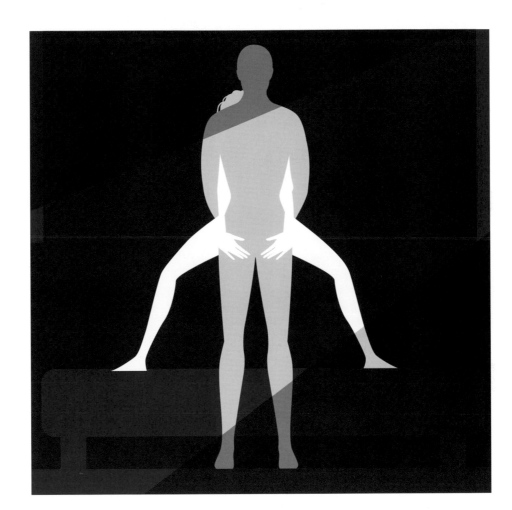

SAUCY SPOONS

Erotic instructions Lie on your sides with him behind you so you're both facing the same direction. Push your butt toward him as he enters you. Put your hand on his and show him how you want your clitoris to be touched. Have him alternate between there and your breasts.

Why you'll love it His hands can explore even the most tucked-away areas of your private parts. And your digits can give him some hands-on instruction, so you get the type of touch you need. Another passion plus: This position is perfect for languorous lovemaking, and the fact that you're so close increases the intimacy.

BUCKING BRONCO

Erotic instructions He lies flat on his back with his knees bent and legs spread apart. Facing him, get on top and slowly lower yourself onto his shaft, keeping your knees bent and your legs outside his arms. Then lean back and support yourself on your palms as he thrusts his hips up and down.

Why you'll love it The angle you create by leaning back is great for G-spot stimulation. Plus, his hands are free to make the rest of your body moan.

The angle you create by leaning backward is good for G-spot stimulation. Meanwhile, his hands are free to roam your entire body.

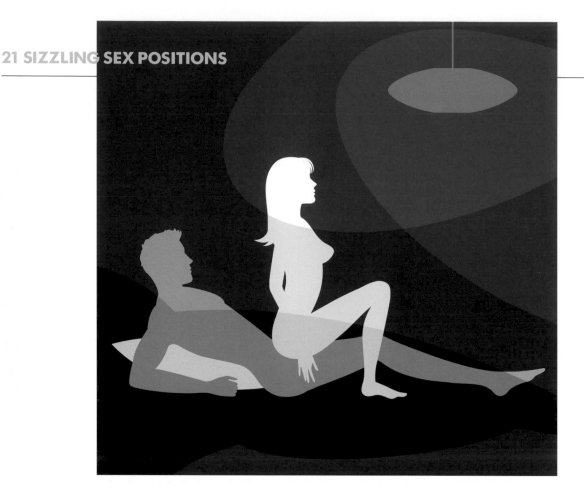

THE REVERSE COWGIRL

Erotic instructions As your guy lies on his back, propped up on his elbows, straddle him facing his feet. Sitting up straight with your hands on his hips, grind into him slowly for a few minutes, building up intense sensations. Then, once you have the ideal angle, you can speed up, letting loose as you vary the depth of penetration. Next, lean back, steadying yourself with your hands (placed next to his sides) until your back presses against his chest. With this change in angle comes a new set of sensations.

Why you'll love it Because there's little eye contact, your man feels free to engage in reckless role-playing, a major turn-on for you both. And when you lean back, he'll be able to caress your breasts, stomach, and clitoris.

WHAT YOUR ORGASM FEELS LIKE TO HIM

Letting loose when he's inside you feels like a series of rapid contractions on his shaft, says Ian Kerner, PhD, author of *She Comes First*. So he'll experience your body tightening and releasing at warp speed. He'll also feel you "upsucking," which is an actual suction effect that happens biologically in order to pull in semen.

To give you a mental picture, here are some analogies: Imagine that your vagina is sucking up a spaghetti strand or tapping Morse code on his penis. Another example: the squeeze and release felt when a doctor uses one of those sleeves to measure blood pressure.

152

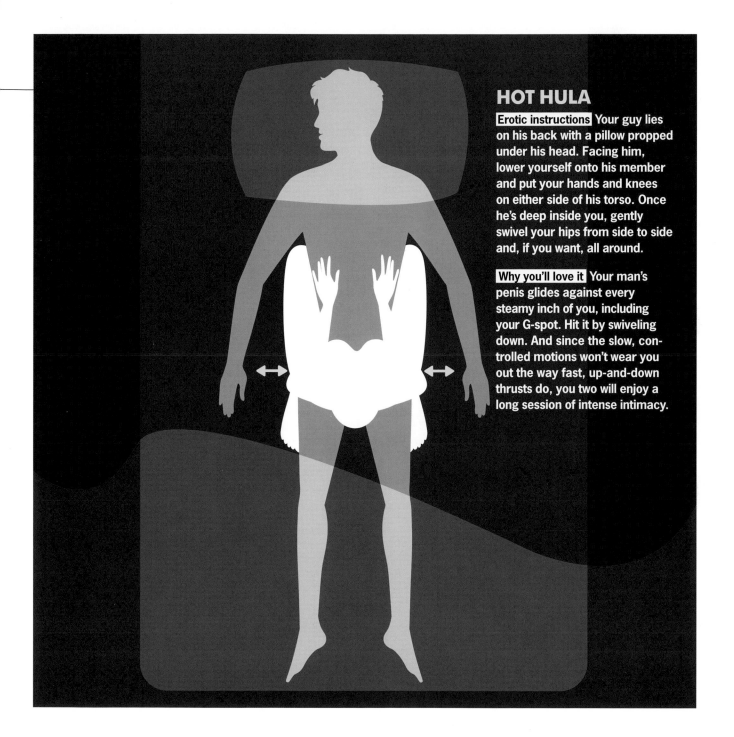

HOT HULA

Erotic instructions Your guy lies on his back with a pillow propped under his head. Facing him, lower yourself onto his member and put your hands and knees on either side of his torso. Once he's deep inside you, gently swivel your hips from side to side and, if you want, all around.

Why you'll love it Your man's penis glides against every steamy inch of you, including your G-spot. Hit it by swiveling down. And since the slow, controlled motions won't wear you out the way fast, up-and-down thrusts do, you two will enjoy a long session of intense intimacy.

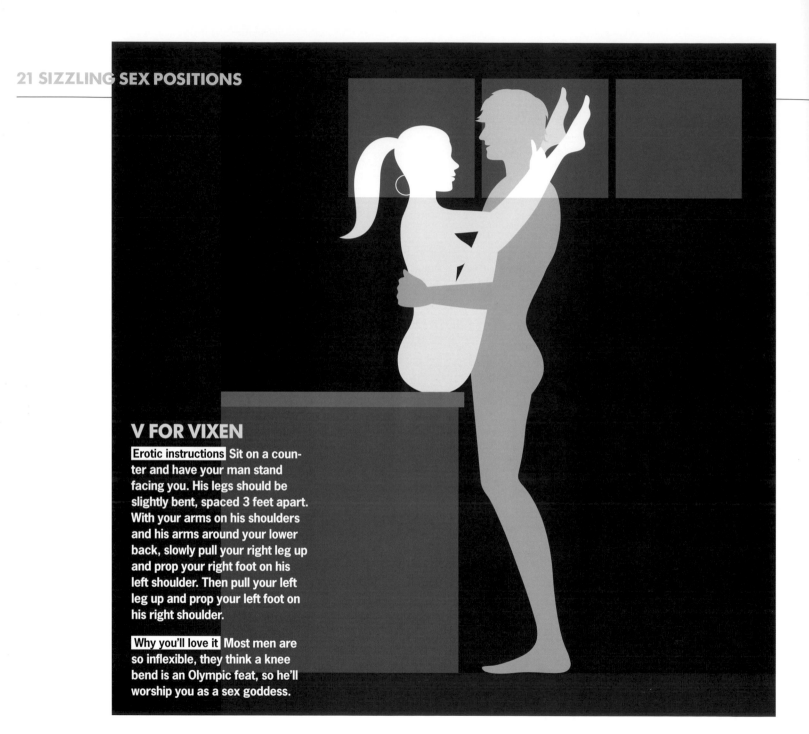

V FOR VIXEN

Erotic instructions Sit on a counter and have your man stand facing you. His legs should be slightly bent, spaced 3 feet apart. With your arms on his shoulders and his arms around your lower back, slowly pull your right leg up and prop your right foot on his left shoulder. Then pull your left leg up and prop your left foot on his right shoulder.

Why you'll love it Most men are so inflexible, they think a knee bend is an Olympic feat, so he'll worship you as a sex goddess.

THE DIRTY DANGLE

Erotic instructions Begin by lying on your back at the foot end of the bed. Have him mount you missionary style and when you're both close to climax, inch toward the edge of the bed until your head, shoulders, and arms hang backward over the side. Then tell him to keep on thrusting.

Why you'll love it The blood will rush to your head, so you can experience erotic inversion, and send tingles to your upper body that will turn your climax into an otherworldly experience. Just don't maintain this position if you feel too light-headed. Passing out from pleasure sounds like a good idea, but it's not meant to be literal.

Create a Signature Sex Move

To claim great-in-bed status, you need to come up with a carnal maneuver that's so creative it deserves to be trademarked. Being treated to a move he's never experienced in quite the same way before is what sears you into a guy's brain.

Here's how to go about concocting a signature technique: First, think of yourself as a carnal athlete—you want to be a champ, so capitalize on your strongest skills.

For example, if you're superflexible, start imagining a sex position that plays to your ability to do a split or put your leg behind your head. Acting naughty is your forte? Make it a practice to give your guy's butt a firm swat at some designated time, such as the moment he peaks.

Just like any other invention, it takes some trial and error to come up with something so great that you (and your bed mate) can't imagine life before it came along. Also, it stands to reason that the more you're into doing something, the more oomph you'll give it.

So if you're ardent about being on top, hop on and find a special signature rocking rhythm (such as a diamond-patterned motion) that he's never been treated to. Do you like man handling? Work out a wrist flick that turns a ho-hum hand job into an award-winning performance. Once you stumble on something that makes both your motors rev, repeat it again and again. Soon your unique technique will be engraved in his memory permanently.

FOR ADVANCED LOVERS

BOOTYFUL VIEW

Erotic instructions Have your man sit up on the bed so that his legs are extended horizontally toward the foot of the bed. Turn around and straddle him—with your back toward him—and then lower yourself onto his erect penis. Extend your legs back so they are almost behind him, relaxing your torso onto the bed between his feet. Slide up and down and use his feet for leverage.

Why you'll love it This position allows for great control over speed, depth, and intensity of stimulation. Since you're facing away, you can feel totally uninhibited, and your partner can enjoy the thrill of the ride.

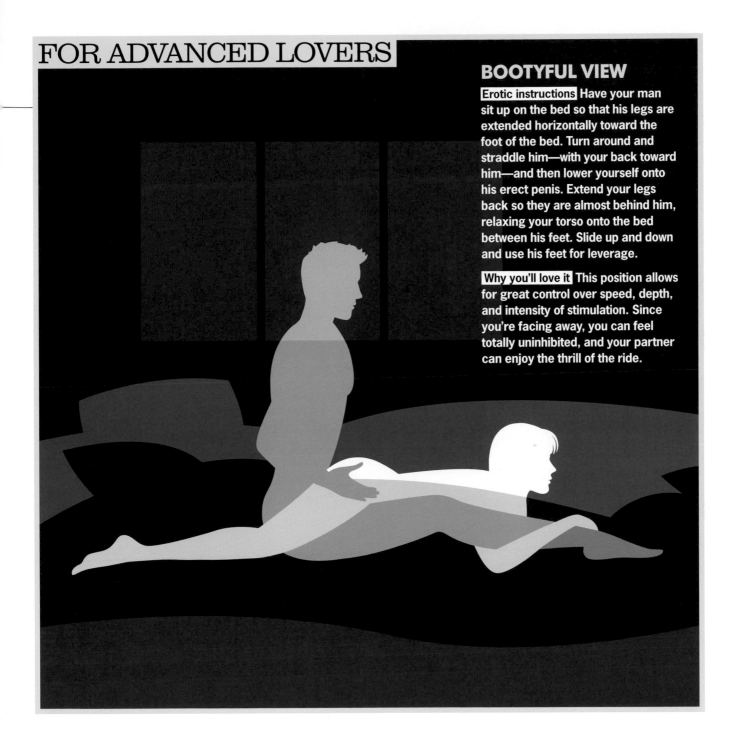

Slowing down a guy when he's close to climaxing will make his orgasm even stronger.

Secrets to Maximizing His Climax

▶ When a guy is getting close to climax, he becomes intensely focused on achieving that goal of release. But by prolonging his excitement, you'll actually be guaranteeing him greater pleasure in the form of a longer, stronger orgasm, says Patricia Taylor, PhD, author of *Expanded Orgasm*.

Since he's going to be pretty single-minded at that moment, you'll have to be the one who slows things down. Sometimes you may even have to interrupt the action so he can last as long as possible—and have a more explosive climax. Vera Bodansky, PhD, coauthor of *The Illustrated Guide to Extended Massive Orgasm*, reveals this secret trick: "During

159

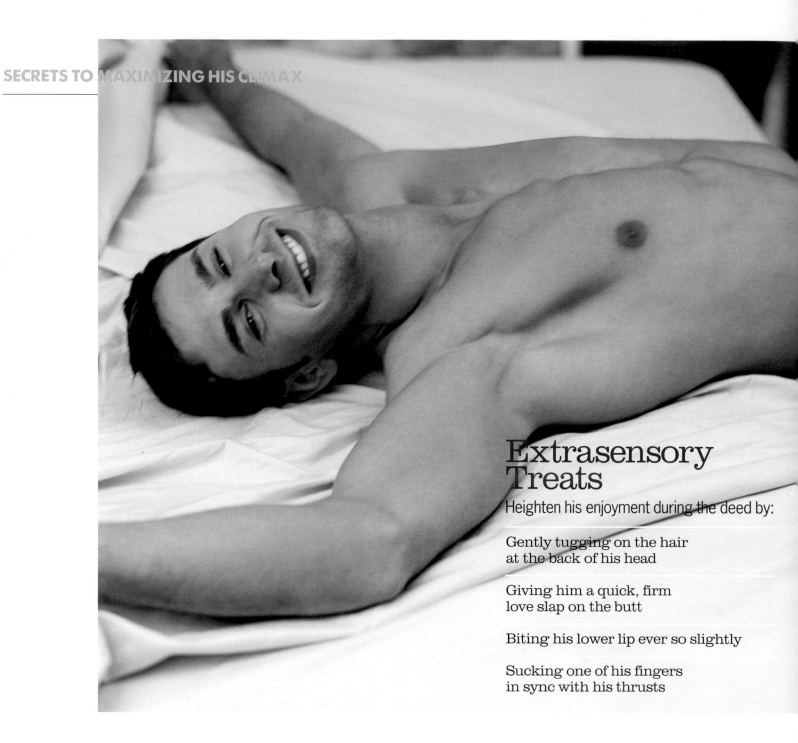

Extrasensory Treats

Heighten his enjoyment during the deed by:

Gently tugging on the hair
at the back of his head

Giving him a quick, firm
love slap on the butt

Biting his lower lip ever so slightly

Sucking one of his fingers
in sync with his thrusts

intercourse, when you sense he's about to ejaculate, have him pull out and firmly squeeze the head of his penis for about four seconds (warn him before you do this)." Then start stimulating him in a different way by switching to oral sex, but lick instead of sucking and avoid the sensitive head.

Another way to take him down to a simmer: When a man is close to climaxing, his testicles contract and pull upward. "To calm him now so that he comes harder later, hold his testicles and massage them downward: With one hand, put your thumb and index finger around the base of his testicles, and with the other hand, caress them with light circular motions," says Margot Anand, author of *The New Art of Sexual Ecstasy*. Certain positions, like woman-on-

DIRTY TALK PRIMER

Put simply, men love dirty talk. They want to hear you say things to them in bed that you'd never utter for anyone else. Some tips on how to get started:

● **Listen to dialogue in an X-rated video. Rewind and play again, noting the words and phrases you find most provocative. Try them on your guy the next time you're getting it on.**

● **Whisper play-by-play descriptions of his—and your—every erotic move in real time.**

● **Tell him no one's ever made you feel this way before.**

● **Vocalize without using words: moan, purr, growl, coo....**

● **Describe his penis using any of the following words: *big, huge, enormous, massive*.**

What to Do When He Finishes Too Fast

About 20 percent of men ages 18 to 59 in the U.S. experience premature ejaculation (PE)—climaxing before both partners wish during intercourse, oral sex, or manual stimulation—on a chronic basis. Some guys who suffer from PE experience more intense sensations and therefore get uncontrollably excited; others orgasm too soon due to performance anxiety (stress causes adrenaline and dopamine to rise, making a man more aroused and less in control of his climax). Another culprit: masturbation. Men focus on finishing fast when pleasuring themselves since climaxing is the goal, so they get conditioned to rapid ejaculation.

Slow-Him-Down Strategy

Stick to the girl-on-top pose. It involves less genital friction and rapid thrusting, which pushes many men over the edge. Also, when you're in control, you can pause for a few seconds if your man's teetering on the edge (ask him to give you a signal). Keep doing this and eventually he will learn more restraint.

SOURCES: SEX THERAPIST IAN KERNER, PHD; JAMES BARADA, MD, DIRECTOR OF THE ALBANY CENTER FOR SEXUAL HEALTH

top, are also effective for prolonging intercourse and delaying ejaculation because *you* control the rate and depth of penetration. Experiment to find the best "cool down" pose.

When you're ready to bring your man back to the boiling point, allow him to resume control of the pace by switching to

The girl-on-top position allows you to maintain control of the pace.

missionary or doggie-style. Right before the big finale, he may increase the rate of his thrusting, and his legs and feet may tense up and even twitch. Here's what's happening inside him at that moment: Several glands in his sex system—including the prostate and the

testicles—emit fluid into the urethra, creating a feeling of fullness and an urge to ejaculate, and the opening to his bladder closes. A few seconds later, his semen is propelled out of the urethra by contractions that hit him every eight-tenths of a second. Even his butt participates: The sphincter muscles contract concurrently with the muscles in his penis.

You can enhance this pleasurable phase by massaging his perineum (the nerve-packed spot between the anus and scrotum). Use the flat part of your finger to treat this area to firm but gentle rhythmic pushes. ■

THE JOYS OF LUBE

There's one widely accepted rule of thumb when it comes to sex: Wetter is better. So even if you don't suffer from vaginal dryness, you should still try using a water-based lube, aka personal lubricant.

The benefits: Being extra lubricated allows your guy to thrust more vigorously without hurting you, making both of you less inhibited. Plus, your below-the-belt sensitivity will skyrocket, enhancing your chances of climaxing. "It acts like a bridge that transfers—and increases—the pleasurable sensations you feel on your skin deep down to your nerve endings," says Hilda Hutcherson, MD, author of *What Your Mother Never Told You About Sex.*

And only a dollop will do ya. "Your vagina should be slick but not so wet that you lose sensation," says Carol Queen, PhD. Three or four drops on your private parts will aid penetration without causing you to lose tightness.

PICKING THE PERFECT LUBE

DON'T USE Anything oil-based (including skin lotion, petroleum jelly, and massage oil) is off-limits, especially to condom users. Oil can leave a rubber as holey as Swiss cheese, rendering it useless for STD and pregnancy protection. And it's safer to steer clear of flavored and colored products, most of which contain irritating chemicals.

DO USE Lubes that are water- or silicone-based. Two good drugstore options: Astroglide and K-Y Liquid (a lighter version of the standard K-Y Jelly).

Even Hotter Action

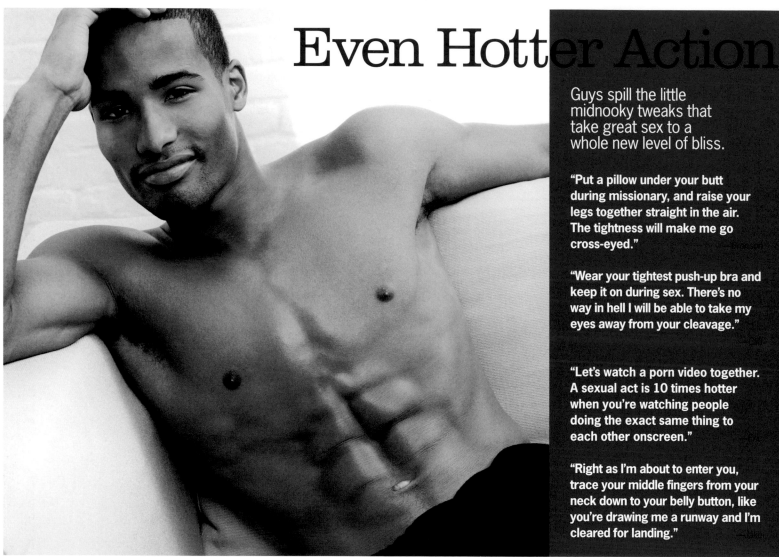

Guys spill the little midnooky tweaks that take great sex to a whole new level of bliss.

"Put a pillow under your butt during missionary, and raise your legs together straight in the air. The tightness will make me go cross-eyed." —Bronson

"Wear your tightest push-up bra and keep it on during sex. There's no way in hell I will be able to take my eyes away from your cleavage." —Cliff

"Let's watch a porn video together. A sexual act is 10 times hotter when you're watching people doing the exact same thing to each other onscreen."

"Right as I'm about to enter you, trace your middle fingers from your neck down to your belly button, like you're drawing me a runway and I'm cleared for landing." —Jake

"One night, play soft and sweet. The next, be rough and aggressive. Mixing it up like that drives me nuts with anticipation. It's almost like being with two different women."
—Arturo

"When we're doing it doggie-style, tell me to stay still while you move back and forth. I won't last very long, but it'll feel amazing ."
—Hank

"There's nothing sexier than a woman who isn't embarrassed about really letting loose when she's having an orgasm."
—Jamal

"Going fast and hard isn't always what the guy wants. Try the 10-second rule: Tell him to enter you and then count to 10 before letting him thrust. He'll feel 10 times the sensation."
—Nelson

"Let me lift your legs over my shoulders during missionary. I can get deeper inside you and rub against your clitoris."
—Ben

"When we're having you-on-top sex, hover so that only the tip of my penis is touching you. Then, without warning, lower yourself so that I plunge into you."
—Dennis

"At the moment I orgasm, alternate between kissing me hard, then licking my lips. It's a complete sensory overload but in a great way."

"Raise your arms over your head when you're lying back during missionary position so I can watch your breasts jiggle around."

"When we're doing it doggie-style, reach back and stroke my inner thighs, the base of my penis—whatever you can reach!"

"Turn off the air conditioning or crank up the heat. Hot and sweaty sex is so primal and animalistic."

"Reverse cowgirl is even steamier when a woman places her feet on my thighs and reaches back to put her hands on my chest. I get to go deep, but she has control."

"Open your legs wide so I can go deep. Bring them together, then spread them again. Constantly shifting position will switch up the sensations I experience."

What he sees is *almost* as good as what he gets.

Give Him a Visual Thrill

▶ You already know men get turned on by visual stimuli. What you may not realize is how powerfully you can amp up your guy's pleasure by exploiting his innate craving for eye candy. "The link between what men see and sexual arousal is an evolutionary holdover from prehistoric times, when the first guy to spot a responsive female was the one who got to mate with her," says certified sexologist Robert W. Birch, PhD.

Thankfully, courtship has progressed since then, but there's still a part of a man's brain that strongly responds to an optical thrill at any stage of seduction, including during the act. Whip these tricks out in bed and he'll go bug-eyed. Oh, and leave the lights on!

167

■ Grab his hand and use it to stimulate all of your hot spots, leaving an arm's length between you so he can see your body and face as your arousal increases.

■ Prop a mirror in front of your bed or a chair, have your guy sit down, then straddle him and get busy. Being able to watch the action—combined with the intoxicating sight of you from behind—will send him completely over the edge.

■ Have him lie back on the bed, straddle him, then *sloowly* lower yourself over his face so he can pleasure you with his mouth. You get oral action, and he gets to see you up close and very personal.

■ Get into 69 position lying on your sides, but instead of having him do any work, encourage him to rest his head on your inner thigh and just enjoy the scenery.

168

Use his hand to stimulate your hot spots, leaving an arm's length between you so he can see your bod and face.

■ Don't take it all off just yet. Keep on a piece of clothing, like a skirt or your bra—or even just a pair of superhigh heels—to give your interlude a couldn't-wait-to-strip-down urgency.

■ In reverse cowgirl, use your hands to support yourself. Then arch your back and drop your head slowly behind you, letting your hair spill across his chest. And if you're really limber, try leaning back and keep stretching until you make eye contact with him upside down. Now that's an X-rated image

he'll never forget...nor would he ever want to.

■ When you're on top, alternate between bouncing up and down so he can see your breasts bobbing and rubbing your hands all over your torso and boobs, squeezing them together to create super cleavage. Even if he's not a boob man, this move will likely turn him into one. ■

SOURCES: CERTIFIED SEXOLOGIST ROBERT W. BIRCH, PHD; LADAWN BLACK, AUTHOR OF *LET'S GET IT ON*; PSYCHOLOGIST AND SEX THERAPIST JOEL D. BLOCK, PHD, AUTHOR OF *THE ART OF THE QUICKIE*; JOAN ELIZABETH LLOYD, AUTHOR OF *HOT SUMMER NIGHTS*

OFFER HIM AN EYEFUL OUTSIDE THE BEDROOM

Wake up a few minutes before the alarm and start getting dressed. This way, he'll catch a glance of you wearing nothing but your bra and panties in the morning, when his testosterone is at its daily peak.

At a meal, slowly and seductively lick a dab of food off your lips or finger. He'll start mentally conjuring up images of what that tongue would feel like all over his naked body.

Wear a piece of jewelry that draws attention to your sexiest parts, like a long necklace that falls in the center of your cleavage or a belly-button ring to bring his gaze down south.

Get undressed in another room, but make sure you're in his line of sight. He'll feel like he's sneaking a forbidden peek of you stripping down.

This is one to-do list you won't mind making.

7 Kinds of Sex All Couples Need

▶ To keep sex exciting, you have to rotate different lovemaking modes through your bedroom repertoire. After all, why limit your experiences to standard fare when there's a whole sensual smorgasbord to sample? Besides, mixing up your sex routine brings mystery and adventure to your love life, two qualities that keep things fresh between the sheets. Start by indulging in these seven sex styles.

171

TAKE-YOUR-SWEET-TIME SEX

When you have the gift of time, languishing in supersensory, soulful lovemaking can be a rhapsodic revelation...and a relationship booster. With sensual sex, it's not all about where you and your guy are going but the process that gets you there. "When you slow down and attempt to keep your orgasm at bay, you're more focused on exploring every inch of each other's bodies and savoring your time together," says Deb Levine, author of *The Joy of Cybersex*.

The emotional benefits are long-lasting too. "Knowing that he cares enough to lavish his love on you for hours, and that you're his number one priority, builds confidence and security," says Levine. "Plus, your bond in general will feel more intimate because you've made the bedroom a place for enjoying each other, not just sexual sensations."

"When you slow down, you're more focused on exploring every inch of each other's bodies."

See if you can beat your own best time.

LIGHT-SPEED SEX

A quickie is kind of like an earthquake: It gets your adrenaline rushing, is over in a flash, and leaves you weak in the knees. Besides releasing your pent-up

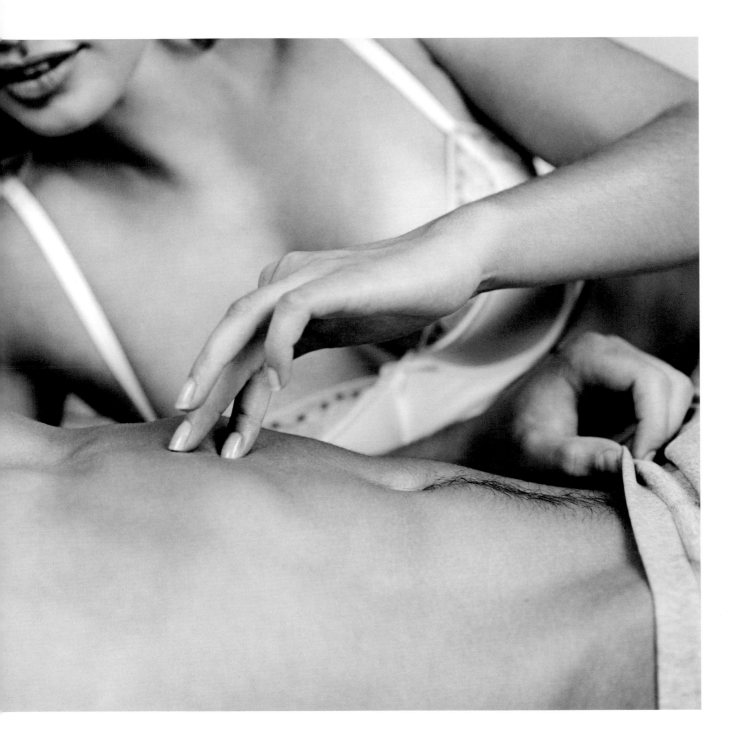

7 New Places to Have Great Sex

1 A Golf Course
Explore the outskirts of the course for a thunderstorm shelter. These shedlike structures are usually placed in remote areas and, unless it starts to pour, no one's going near them. You may also want to sport a cute little golf skirt to allow for easy access.

2 In Front of the Fridge
Open the door to the refrigerator and have your man sit on the floor with his back against the cool shelves. Then straddle him. Not only will the cold air give you both a thrill, but you can also incorporate food into your frisky play.

3 A Rowboat
Rent a boat and row it out to an area free of people. Once there, get into missionary position, which allows you both to stay low (to avoid capsizing the boat with all that rocking!) and out of view—and then try to make some waves of your own.

4 The Hood of Your Car
You can put a new spin on a classic hookup spot by getting out of the backseat and climbing on top of your ride. Spread a blanket on the hood, and have an old-school romp under the stars.

5 A Farmer's Field
Have sex in the tall grass by the side of the road when you're taking a spin in the country.

6 A Sleeping Compartment on a Train
If you've ever wanted to make out in a moving vehicle, a train is the way to go. You'll have to pay a little extra to get your own berth, but the private area will be your passion playground. All aboard!

7 An Exercise Bench
Have a home gym? Use it to work up a sweat. The bench is the right balance of firm and soft, plus it puts you in perfect alignment for girl-on-top sex. Have him lie down, then lower yourself on top of him, using your legs to move up and down.

lust, initiating a quickie can be the ultimate compliment to your guy because it shows how deeply you desire him.

In addition, when he's had a stressful day, a fast and furious romp really takes the edge off. Put simply: "Sometimes guys want to take their time, and sometimes they just want to get their rocks off," says William Fitzgerald, PhD, a retired sex therapist in San Jose, California. When you can tell he's in a horny, hasty mood, don't bother fully undressing—just pull his penis out of the opening in his boxers and push your panties

aside. All you need for successful speed sex is lube, says Los Angeles sex therapist Donald Etkes, PhD. "It's your best friend when you don't have time to get completely warmed up."

Take your star turn...or at least pretend to.

SHOW-OFF SEX

You may think it would be easier to give a speech in the presence of 500 people than to masturbate in front of your man, but

taking that plunge may be worth it—experts say that watching a woman pleasure herself is near the top of most men's fantasy wish lists. But it's not just a very personal peep show; it's a chance to teach him exactly how you like to be manhandled.

Revealing to your guy how you master your own domain is one of the most secretive and intimate things you can do.

Kick this guy out of bed before you get started.

COMFORT SEX

Anyone with a pulse would be crazy not to crave a hot-and-spicy sack session. But sometimes all you want is the sexual equivalent of mac and cheese: It may not be exciting, but it

If one of you has had a particularly bad day, fast and furious sex does an incredible job of taking the edge off.

makes you feel so good. "People have sex for a lot of different reasons, and one of them is to be soothed and comforted," says Chicago marital-sex therapist Michael Seiler, PhD. "Making each other feel loved and cared for is the most powerful way to bring the psychological and physical elements of your relationship together."

Let him see your animalistic side.

WILD-KINGDOM SEX

It's the raw, primal, grunting kind of sex that wakes the neighbors, scares house pets, and rattles bed frames—the more writhing and bucking, the better.

Any animalistic sex session starts, fittingly, on all fours (aka doggie-style). Grab his hands and wrap them around your waist—a cue that you want him to hold on and thrust—and he'll answer your call of the wild. Keep your neck down. It'll help you loosen up all the way down your spine so you can move your tush with gusto.

SURRENDER SEX

Men are conquest-loving creatures, which is why they get so hot when you let them take over. "If he feels like he's at the top of his game, your surrender

6

is a power trip and a huge turn-on," says Fitzgerald.

During foreplay, let your legs fall open and hold the headboard or pillows above you so your whole body is exposed to him. Then invite him to slide on top of you. Meet his thrusts halfway by rocking your pelvis upward against his and lifting your legs in the air with your feet spread far apart. This gives him room to maneuver his body and alternate between deep thrusting and short pumping. Then drape your legs over his shoulders so he can grab your ankles and posi-

tion them where he wants them. "Tell him you want him to make you come," says Etkes. "It says that you want him running the show because he has the skills to get you there."

He won't mind if you act like a control freak.

FEMALE-DOMINATION SEX

If he's been doing all the pouncing and pawing lately, take the reins. But a truly titillating

takeover has to be authentic and not staged, so wait until you're really randy, straddle him, and say, "I'd love to be in charge tonight." Then gently grab his penis and rub it around your clitoris as if he were your personal sex toy.

Once you slip him in, pin his hands to the bed or tie him to the headboard with scarves or stockings while you grind against his lap in a circular motion. Or try this hot move: Stick your breasts in his face and instruct him to flick your nipples with his tongue—the only part of him that's free to move. He'll happily submit to your sexy request.

Another in-command position: girl-on-top 69. Rub your hot spot against his tongue and pivot your hips back and forth in sync with the lip service you're giving him. ■

In order for it to feel authentic, wait until you're really randy, then straddle him and say, "I'd love to take charge tonight."

When You Want It More Than He Does

▶ Rumor has it that men are always in heat. But passion levels vary by individual due to an array of physiological and psychological factors. And there are more than a few women who are frustrated by their man's lagging libido. Understandably, chicks facing this situation say that it's tough not to take a partner's disinterest personally. So what's at the root of a stalled sex drive? Following, some reasons—and possible resolutions.

He's lost that lovin' feeling. Now what?

THE THRILL IS GONE

When that frenzied early-dating lust dies down and you've eased into the comfort zone, the desire chasm often widens between men and women. The cruel carnal irony: Females tend to become more uninhibited as their trust in a lover increases over time while men crave the proverbial thrill of the chase.

Hereditary Horniness

University students who described their sex drives as subdued were found to have a different variation of a specific gene than students who reported having higher libidos, according to a study published in the journal *Molecular Psychiatry*.

Though the study shows that nature plays a role in arousal, your libido isn't totally predetermined by your family history. "Other factors, like the culture in which you were raised and how you feel about your partner, also affect the level of your desire," explains study coauthor Richard Ebstein, PhD, director of the Scheinfeld Center for Human Genetics in the Social Sciences at the Hebrew University of Jerusalem.

But familiarity doesn't have to breed boredom. Some fixes: Take turns being the giver and the receiver. When you're completely focused on the other person and not your own pleasure, it allows you to explore and find new hot buttons.

HE'S TOTALLY STRESSED OUT

Day-to-day interferences such as work pressures, cash-flow concerns, and family responsibilities rank at the top of the list of hot-sex wreckers. If you sense that something is eating at your man, don't push him to talk about it—or for sex. Instead, take the pressure off by giving him a massage or just being affectionate. It may stop there, but the understanding and physical attention could end up arousing him.

YOU'VE LET YOURSELF GO

Okay, this is gonna sting a little: Love may be unconditional, but attraction isn't. If you've gained a lot of weight and think he's not wild about your shape anymore, you need to do something about it. Join a gym. Cook healthier meals. Exercise together—go for a run, and then join him for a hot, steamy, post-workout shower.

On the other hand, if his physique is the one that's gone downhill, it could be doing a number on his ego, which would definitely dampen his sex drive. Or he could be sluggish in the sack because he's living on a diet of energy-draining fast food. Either way, take heart—weight and energy issues can be overcome with a little discipline and desire.

HIS SEX DRIVE IS SET ON LOW

"To some degree, sex drives are set biologically," explains Lonnie Barbach, PhD, author of *For Each Other*. That said, most libidos do have a tendency to ebb and flow over the course of a lifetime, so if your sex drives don't gel, you may have to live with it for a little while… or forever.

But first, determine if his lack of interest might possibly be due to some kind of medical problem, such as depression, anxiety, or even a heart condition. And some medications (such as certain antidepressants, which can have libido-dampening side effects) could be curbing his sexual appetite. Try to convince him to have a complete physical to rule out any physiological problems. ■

3 LUST BUSTERS

Certain lifestyle habits and changes can put a damper on women's sex drives.

1 Smoking
Nicotine in cigarettes reduces the size of your blood vessels, and blood flow to your nether regions is what arousal is all about. So stop smoking and learn to breathe in a way that increases oxygen flow and circulation.

2 Boozing
Everyone knows that drinking alcohol in small quantities can have an aphrodisiacal effect, but moderate to excessive imbibing can impact estrogen levels and libido.

3 Breast Feeding
Some new moms report a shift in the way they view the sexual parts of their bodies after childbirth. Vaginal muscles are stretched, and sex may be painful due to tissue that is still healing. Plus, when your breasts are being used as a baby buffet, it can be hard to think of them as pleasure receptors.

Take Sex to a Deeper Level

> Physical pleasure and satisfaction are a major part of the payoff when you have sex. But emotional connection counts too, and it's nice to make room in your repertoire for more soulful encounters, where bonding with your mate is as much the focus as getting off is (well, almost). Not to get all corny on you, but savoring every sexual touch and sensation during a sensual night between the sheets can magnify the emotional as well as the physical experience of sex.

Start by lying in bed in a face-to-face position just kissing and caressing. This mutual stimulation will likely put you in a meditative state, allowing you to zero in on each sensation. Let your hands glide down his spine and over his buttocks. He'll instinctively start touching

This kind of lovemaking will bring you closer to him...inside the bedroom and out.

you in a similar way. As you stroke each other, sync up your breathing by inhaling and exhaling, slowly and deliberately. (You can clue him in to what you're doing or simply wait to see if he naturally follows suit.) Breathing in tandem helps your excitement levels rise at the same rate, which makes you feel physically melded during sex, says New York City sex therapist Joy Davidson, PhD.

You can intensify all this sensory enjoyment by preventing yourself from seeing and hearing distracting sights and noises, which also keeps you totally centered on the moment and each other. To get into concentration mode, ditch the music and dim the lights. You need total silence and near darkness. By deleting one or two senses, the others become much more acute, so pleasurable touches feel even more so.

As you start fooling around, really take in how your guy feels, tastes, and smells. Notice the texture of his skin, listen to his pounding heart as his arousal escalates, and nuzzle him all over so you can inhale

Breathing in tandem helps your excitement levels rise at the same rate, which makes you feel physically melded.

his essence. Try not to make a single peep, save for a few moans and sighs that mindlessly escape your lips. At the same time, allow yourself to become lost in everything he's doing to you. Just relax and revel in the exquisite pleasure of being with your partner.

If you're not into the idea of fondling each other in the dark, there's another technique that can fuse you: Gazing into your partner's eyes (stop laughing!). We're not advising that you get into a staring contest—it's more like you're looking inside him rather than just at him. Study his facial expression and try to imagine what he's thinking and feeling, especially when he's nearing orgasm. There's something so soul baring about seeing your partner at that instant, when he's at his most open and vulnerable…and letting him see you. ■

HAVE SLEEPY SEX
Getting it on first thing in the a.m. can be incredibly sensual, because you're half conscious so you're acting more on instinct.

Peaking Together

You've just read about how to have superconnected sex, but there's one aspect of that deeper kind of love that we haven't hit upon: achieving simultaneous orgasms. It's one of the most gratifying sexual experiences you can have with a guy you're in love with—and even with one you never plan to see again! But simultaneous Os can be tricky to achieve.

For many women, it's easier to climax from oral sex and manual stimulation. But to orgasm in tandem with your man, you first need to learn to climax when you have intercourse. "It may be easier

easier to peak during oral or manual because he's focused on your clitoris," explains Ava Cadell, PhD. "In many positions, you won't achieve clitoral stimulation unless you consciously create contact."

Begin by recreating the sensations you feel during oral and manual action. Use extra lube to imitate the warmth and wetness of his mouth. Also, start slowly. "Let him enter you only halfway in the beginning, simulating the shallow penetration from his mouth or hands," suggests Ian Kerner, PhD.

As he goes deeper, touch yourself so you're stimulated on the inside *and* outside. With a little practice, climaxing during intercourse will come naturally.

Once you're primed for peaking during the act, you need to work on your timing. Since men tend to climax faster than women do, get a head start. Have him tantalize you manually or orally for 10 minutes so you're close to the edge. Once you're ready for intercourse, opt for the woman-on-top position so you can control the pace. "Rub your clitoris in circles to get more blood flowing there," says Cadell. If he's nearing the O zone too quickly, "pull away so only the tip of his penis is inside you and make shallow movements," says Kerner. This downshifts his arousal while giving you intense clitoral stimulation.

If he's just moments away, stop having sex, and gently squeeze the head of his member for about four seconds (remember this nifty little trick from page 161?). Squeezing quickly halts the blood flow to his penis, successfully abating arousal.

If he still blasts off before you, don't get discouraged. The more often you try climaxing together, the easier it will become.

Scorching In-the-Act Sex Tips

Wanna make a lusty and lasting impression? Bust out these moves.

"Make me explode during doggie-style sex by turning your face to the side and making out with me."

"The first time we sleep together, do something a little taboo. It's like, who is this new girl? She looked so sweet when I first met her. Except don't call me Daddy...that's weird."

"Talk dirty by telling me exactly what you want me to do to you. It fills me in on what you love the most, but it also just sounds so damn hot."

"Squeeze my biceps and triceps while we're doing it missionary-style. It makes me feel like a strong macho man."

"During sex, firmly hold the base of my penis while I'm thrusting in and out. It really increases friction."

"While we're changing positions, give me an oral-sex break. It lasts mere seconds, but it's really unbelievable."

"Gasp or moan heavily when I enter you. It makes me feel really big, and that's such a turn-on for me."

"Tease me. Get on top and bounce really fast. Then slow down. Once the tension is built up, sit on my lap and grind. The penetration is so deep that I can feel your vagina gripping my penis from the tip to the base. It's sort of like I'm hitting a wall inside you."

"Spooning has a tame rep, but it's so hot. I can get really deep, play with my girl's breasts, and feel her backside buck against my hips. It's total body pleasure."

"Once, a girl told me to lie still while she was on top. Then she turned an entire 360 degrees with me inside her. I felt every inch of her."

"Start in missionary, then put one leg between mine and the other on my shoulder. You'll end up on your side, giving me a view of your breasts and butt at the same time."

"Once I've come, keep moving your hips and squeezing your PC muscles. It's an amazing after-sex feeling that stretches out my pleasure."

"My lady likes to lie facedown, with her legs straight and her arms at her sides. To enter her, I have to push past her legs and cheeks. The resistance is really hot."

"While I'm on top, lift yourself up a bit and gently bite my nipple or lick my neck. It lets me know you're into things and having fun."

"Any man will tell you that it's a turn-on if he sees you watching him moving in and out of you. So let me catch you looking."

"In doggie-style, sway your hips in a circle. I don't get to see you move like that often enough."

Once you've mastered that first peak, the climb to the next one is absolutely attainable.

Aiming for Multiple Orgasms

▶ As we said previously, achieving one orgasm is a huge challenge for some women. But once you've mastered that first peak (and this book will help get you there), the climb to the next one is absolutely obtainable. "The average woman is built to come again and again," says Rachel Carlton Abrams, MD, coauthor of *The Multi-Orgasmic Woman*. "Women don't require a refractory period like men do, so we're able to stay aroused for longer and many of us can orgasm a second and third time." How's that for fab news? There are two common types of multiples: Sequential orgasms, which are a series of roller coaster–like waves that are 2 to 10 minutes apart, and serial orgasms, which are rapid-fire shots of pleasure with only a few seconds of interruption.

To reach that very happy place where either variety of multiples can happen, you've got to make sure you have some time on your hands. One of the biggest misconceptions women have about multiple orgasms is that they happen serendipitously, but like anything else that's worthwhile, they require a little effort and planning.

Start by getting one orgasm under your belt in whatever way is easiest for you (perhaps by having your guy bring you there through clitoral stimulation from oral sex). Climaxing before intercourse means that your body will be geared up to come again and respond to the added vaginal stimulation during sex.

And even if you don't come, receiving oral sex still paves the way for multiples. Ask him to use this technique: He pleasures

you with his tongue for a minute or so before pulling away for a few seconds, then he dives right back in. "This teasing primes the body to expect that after each peak of sensation, another one is coming," says Dr. Abrams. "And it remembers that lesson when you orgasm—after one, your body will stay in that prepped state, putting you on track to climax again."

After an orgasm, a lot of nerve pathways have been stimulated, and there's been a tremendous surge in blood flow, so it's completely natural to want to take a break from stimulation in those moments drains away. Keep up the caressing until you feel that heat returning to your genitals.

Another great route: treat intercourse as a full-contact sport. That means having your lover fondle your breasts or

Receiving oral sex paves the way for multiples...if he uses a certain teasing technique.

immediately following. But if you resume touching an area that is not hypersensitive, you bring on more pleasure.

Give the vaginal area a break for a minute and have your partner kiss you or stroke your breasts. Touching other regions will keep your nerves and sensual energy on high alert while your clitoris's hypersensitivity

trail his nails down your back as you create constant contact by rubbing your clitoris against his body in a rocking motion during girl-on-top sex. "Women are more likely to have additional orgasms if they are stimulating several body parts at the same time," says Dr. Abrams. Your body never quite knows exactly what to expect

next and is more likely to respond, over and over again.

Lastly, put your PC (pubococcygeus) muscles to work (see "Kegels Crash Course" on page 23 for a refresher). "Since your orgasm is essentially an intense contraction of your PC and pelvic floor muscles, strengthening them increases blood flow to the area and enables you to experience deeper orgasms more easily," says Laura Berman, PhD.

You can use your PC strength to move beyond the initial climax into the euphoric realm (yes, it's *that* good) by pumping your muscles in small bursts when you feel that first orgasm. Doing that draws out that initial pleasure wave and creates momentum for the next series of orgasmic contractions. ■

Kinky-Lite Play She Craves

1 Rougher Touches

While sweet, soulful lovemaking is all well and good, every now and then your woman may want to be manhandled a bit. Why? Because it's erotic for a woman to be thrown down on the bed, since it lets her know that you're hot for her and can't wait to have her. Feeling like putty in your hands is the reason we blurt out things in ecstasy like "Take me, I'm yours." Okay, even if you don't do that, you may find the whole power/submission dynamic hot. No wonder those romance novels with the bodice-ripping he-men are so popular.

2 Sight Depravation

Trust us, being blindfolded in bed is something almost every girl wants to experience. Being visionless literally gives her no choice but to channel her concentration and really focus on every

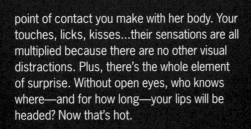

point of contact you make with her body. Your touches, licks, kisses...their sensations are all multiplied because there are no other visual distractions. Plus, there's the whole element of surprise. Without open eyes, who knows where—and for how long—your lips will be headed? Now that's hot.

3 Dangerous Venues

Women need adventure! So take her on a frisky field trip—outside the bedroom. Have sex in the bathroom at a party, your parked car, or—eek!—your parents' place (that will get the blood pumping). Sure it's risky, but that's the point. Just the thrill of being naughty and possibly getting caught will set her panties on fire. Plus, new, uncharted carnal territory will force you to adapt to your surroundings and lock your bods in fresh and exciting ways.

4 The Game "May I?"

Mind your manners and request permission before laying a hand (or lip or tongue) on her body, as in "Can I suck your nipples?" It means that sexual liberties aren't a sure thing and that she has the power to reject you (not that she would). Also, vocalizing words that usually remain unspoken is a tawdry treat in itself.

HER KIND OF DIRTY TALK

Not everything flies when it comes to giving your girl an erotic earful. Here, how to find the words that'll turn her on.

TEST HER OUTSIDE THE BEDROOM
Say something like "I was at the gym, thinking about your hot ass." If she seems intrigued, it's okay to bust out the naughty talk between the sheets. If not, you may have to settle for grunts and moans.

START OFF SMALL
Getting too raunchy too fast could backfire. Ease into it by telling her how aroused she makes you. It is really flattering and helps to cement an image of herself as desirable and alluring.

BE SPECIFIC
Talk about how amazing her breasts look and how you love grasping her firm butt. Detailed compliments let her know that you worship her bod specifically.

TAKE IT UP A NOTCH
If she volleys back with something just as frisky or belts out some keep-it-coming moaning, then tell her that you love the way she tastes and smells.

SOURCE: SEX THERAPIST ALINE P. ZOLDBROD, PHD, COAUTHOR OF *SEX TALK*

PRACTICE MAKES PERFECT
Get comfortable talking dirty by engaging in a little phone sex. The distance feels safer.

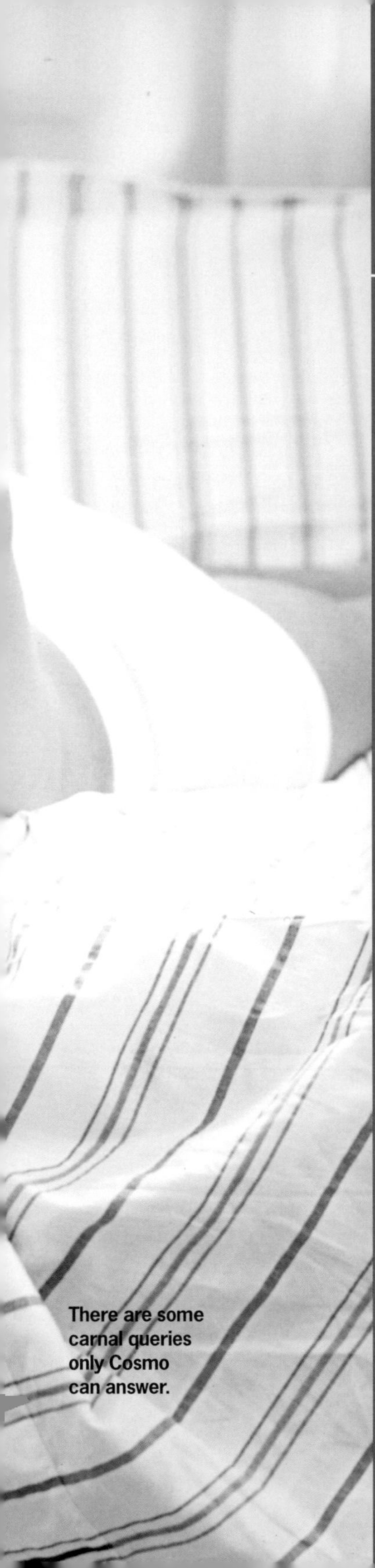

Super Private Sex Questions— Answered

▶ Sex has the potential to be exciting, beautiful, exhila-
rating, and at times, embarrassing and perplexing.
And as any sexually active chick knows, certain things
occur during the act that are too personal to ask even
your closest girlfriends. Besides, in many instances
they wouldn't know the right answers.

But you can always count on Cosmo to give you
candid advice. For proof of that, keep reading as we
share some of the most burning bedroom queries
we've received over the years—and of course, the
reassuring responses.

There are some
carnal queries
only Cosmo
can answer.

195

Q: IS IT REALLY POSSIBLE FOR A MAN'S PENIS TO BREAK?

A: Yes. Called a penile fracture, this ultrapainful injury happens when a guy's erect member is bent sharply or if he accidentally thrusts against a hard surface, such as his partner's thigh or pubic bone. The result: The inner chambers of the penis rupture, causing a popping sound, followed by instant pain, swelling, and bruising.

Should it occur, your guy has to go to an emergency room ASAP. "Without proper medical care, scar tissue can build up as the fracture heals, leading to a permanent penile curve," explains Sheldon Marks, MD, assistant clinical professor of urology at the University of Arizona College of Medicine and WebMD men's health expert.

nal health) can benefit men too. "Males have pubococcygeus (PC) muscles just like females do," explains Marc Goldstein, surgeon-in-chief of male reproductive medicine and surgery at New York–Presbyterian Hospital Weill/Cornell Medical Center

Just like women, men have PC muscles. Strengthening them can help a guy achieve firmer erections.

Q: I HEARD THAT GUYS SHOULD DO KEGELS. IS THIS TRUE?

A: Yes! The very same exercises experts recommend to women to enhance sexual pleasure (and for women, vagi-

in New York City. Strengthening these muscles with Kegels can help men achieve firmer erections and fix premature ejaculation problems, he says. To help your guy locate his PC muscles, tell him to try stopping the flow of urine. He should contract and hold the muscles he uses to do that for three seconds, building up to 26 three-second contractions in a row daily.

Q: I'M HORNY WHEN I HAVE MY PERIOD. IS IT COOL TO HAVE SEX OR WILL I TOTALLY GROSS OUT MY GUY?

A: The only way to be really sure how your man feels is to ask him. If he's game, consider sticking to the missionary position. "Your bleeding may be lighter if you're lying down," says Patricia Taylor, PhD. But if you vary positions, keep your flow at bay by inserting a diaphragm-type menstrual cup (an alternative to tampons and pads that you can buy at a drugstore or online) presex.

Just remember, while there are benefits to doing the deed during your time of the month—some women experience reduced cramping—it *is* possible to get pregnant. Plus, there is a greater chance of HIV transmission, because the virus has easy access to your bloodstream as you shed the lining of your uterus.

Also an option, you could try out one of the types of birth-control pills that are on the market that cause you to skip your period altogether.

197

Approaching the Back Door

These days, interest in back-door booty is growing. Due to the prevalence of online pornography and the breaking down of sexual taboos, anal play is no longer considered something only gay guys participate in.

However, because anal sex still isn't exactly mainstream, the prospect of exploring a somewhat "forbidden" area can be extremely erotic, says Barbara Keesling, PhD. Not to mention the fact that the anus is loaded with nerve endings and can be a pleasure center for both men and women.

If you're game to lavish some attention on your guy's back-door area, proceed with caution until you know how he feels about it.

Some guys consider their anus a no-fly zone. Test the waters by lightly, almost accidentally, grazing a finger over and around the outside of his anus when you're giving him a hand job or oral sex. If he clenches his cheeks and pulls away, then you know he's either too shy to let you go *there* or he's just not into it. If he lifts his butt (or otherwise pushes himself toward your hand) or lets a sigh escape his lips, you can explore a little more.

Apply some lube to your finger then make circular motions around the opening. There are a lot of supersensitive nerve endings in

EXIT ONLY

that region, so touching him there is very likely to bring him bliss. The male G-spot (the prostate gland) is located on the front wall of the rectum, and it can be very pleasurable when stroked. But if you want to go as far as actually inserting your finger, you should probably get his permission first.

If you're aching for him to explore *your* back door, ask him to treat you to those same circular motions (with a lubed finger, of course) around the anus during oral sex or intercourse.

Eager to try full penetration, you tigress? There are a few key things you should be aware of. Unlike the vagina, the anus isn't self-lubricating nor is it as elastic. "The sphincter muscles clench upon contact, making penetration uncomfortable if you're not fully relaxed," says Keesling. So to enjoy the act, you need to take it slowly, having him insert just a little of his penis at a time. And be sure to use lots of lube. Finally, even couples in a monogamous relationship must use a condom (free of nonoxynol-9, which can damage rectal tissue) to prevent the spread of bacteria, and be sure to replace that condom before switching to vaginal intercourse.

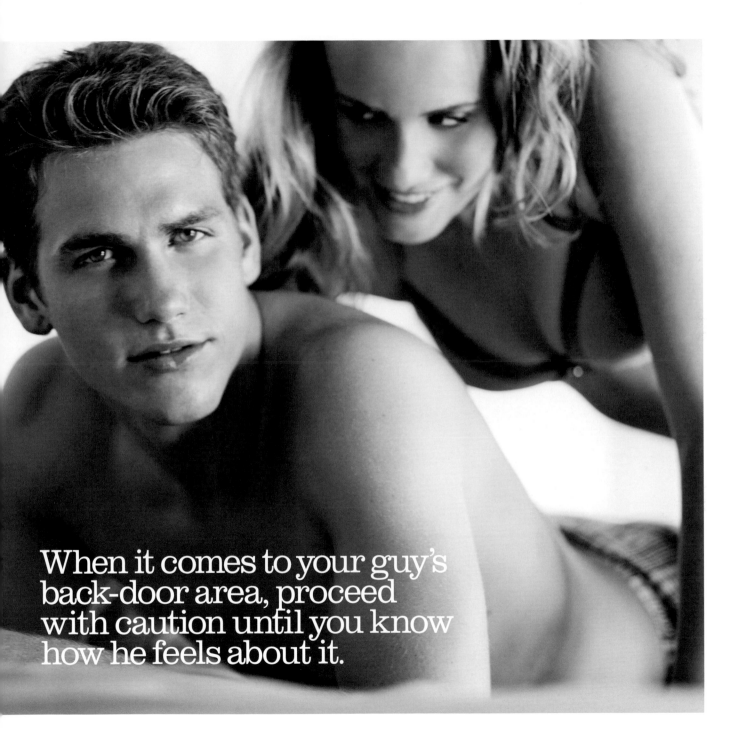

When it comes to your guy's back-door area, proceed with caution until you know how he feels about it.

Q: SOMETIMES WHEN I'M HAVING SEX, MY VAGINA MAKES AN EMBARRASSING NOISE, LIKE I'M PASSING GAS. CAN I PREVENT IT?

A: This noisy emission, commonly referred to as a queef, is air escaping your vagina. "When you're aroused, your vagina expands to allow room for your partner's penis," explains Barbara Keesling, PhD. "His thrusting during intercourse pushes air into you, which fills the space in your vagina that has expanded. A shift in body position or a deep thrust can force that air out, resulting in the fartlike sound." It's also possible to queef post-orgasm, when air is expelled as the vagina returns to its pre-aroused state.

While it's totally normal and very common for this noise to escape your body, if it's getting in the way of your pleasure, try taking these preventive measures: First, "lie on your back and gently press down on your abdomen with the palm of your hand prior to intercourse," suggests Keesling. "This will expel air already present in your vagina." During sex, encourage your guy to make shallow strokes. If you do toot, just try to laugh it off. Any guy worth sleeping with will do the same.

It's totally normal for noises to escape your body during sex. Try to laugh it off. Any guy worth sleeping with will do the same.

Q: I WORRY ABOUT HOW I TASTE AND SMELL WHEN A NEW MAN GOES DOWN ON ME. IS THERE ANYTHING I SHOULD DO ABOUT IT?

A: "Women often worry about how they taste and smell, which is ironic, since many men are actually turned on by the natural aroma of their partners," says Keesling.

However, even if your man thinks you smell as sweet as a rose garden, you won't be able to enjoy his effort fully if you're worried about offending him. Your best bet is to wash your genital region with soap and water before sex (avoid using douches and vaginal deodorants, which can irritate sensitive tissue). Hey, why not take a steamy shower or bath together as part of foreplay?

Even if you don't suds up first, try to relax and focus solely on all the pleasure your man's mouth gives you. If he voluntarily heads downtown and stays there, he's most likely not offended by your scent—in fact, there's a very good chance he loves it.

Q: CAN WOMEN REALLY EJACULATE WHEN THEY CLIMAX?

A: Since fluid is expelled from the urethra upon orgasm, many people think it's a stream of urine, says Sandor Gardos, PhD. However, some researchers believe that at least some of the mystery fluid is produced by the Skene's glands, located on either side of a woman's urethral opening, and may be similar in composition to male ejaculate—minus the sperm, of course.

201

Q: MY BOY-FRIEND AND I USE SEX TOYS. HOW OFTEN DO WE NEED TO WASH THEM?

A: Keep them germ-free by rinsing them right after sex with hot water and a mild antibacterial soap. (If your toy is made from silicone, check the instructions: You may be able to boil it in hot water or stick it in the dishwasher.) If you don't correctly clean your booty buddies after each use, bacteria on the toys can multiply and may trigger a vaginal infection next time you use them, explains Jeanne Marrazzo, MD, associate professor of infectious diseases at the University of Washington. And unless you're sure you and your man are both STD free, slide a condom over the toy before using it so an infection won't be passed on, adds Dr. Marrazzo.

Q: MY GUY PLAYS ROUGH WITH MY RACK. CAN HE DO ANY DAMAGE?

A: The skin on your chest is especially thin and sensitive to the touch, and any man-handling can lead to minor scratches and slight bruising. "But as long as you don't feel excessive pain while your boyfriend fondles your breasts, his roughhousing shouldn't cause anything other than a superficial injury," explains Mitchell Creinin, MD, professor of obstetrics, gynecology, and reproductive sciences at the University of Pittsburgh School of Medicine. Of course, there's always a tiny chance that your guy's aggressive strokes and nibbles will break the skin, which might lead to a bacterial infection of the tissue. So if you detect any swelling or experience persistent pain, check with your doctor. ∎

There is always a tiny chance that your guy's aggressive strokes and nibbles will break sensitive breast skin.

You've heard of afterglow, but chances are, afterplay is a new concept. What is it? Cosmo's term for an array of amorous activities you can—and should—engage in during the seconds, minutes, and hours following a sheet-tangling sex session.

When you think about it, there are few places and times where you and your mate are more physically and emotionally connected to each other than after sex. So why not capitalize on that special time? To help you do just that, we've filled the following pages with sweet and sexy ideas about how to pamper a man after doing the deed (and how to get him to reciprocate that treatment). You'll also find tips on keeping arousal amped in the likely event that you'll want to parlay the postcoital resting period into a sizzling second round. So whether you want to snuggle and get closer or have him twice (or more) in one night, we have advice that will ensure the bedroom fun lives on.

Postsex moments are prime bonding time.

Staying Connected After Sex

▶ Just because the main event is over, that doesn't mean you and your man have to retreat to opposite sides of the bed. Immediately after climax, with your guy still inside you, run your fingers down his back, over his buttocks, and along his sides. Do it in a slow rhythm up and down his back using a wavelike motion. Since most men's backs are very sensitive, it will soothe him.

At this point, guy's egos are supervulnerable. So if there's something he did that drove you insane in a good way, now's the best time to tell him. After tending to his ego, turn your attention back to his body. Turn the pages for some pampering pointers to try.

■ During sex, blood flow in the body rushes to the genitals. As it leaves, even the gentlest touch might be too much pressure for him, but lightly blowing on his package will help cool him off while his body settles down.

■ Most guys have a couple of postsex sweet spots: areas that are receptive to being touched, licked, or kissed. They can be anywhere from his collarbone to the insides of his wrists, where the skin is thinner and more sensitive. Experiment to find his.

■ After he ejaculates, a man's

Men aren't wired to be verbal after having an orgasm, but you can connect without having to speak a word.

sense of smell may be heightened. Light a scented candle that gives off a comforting aroma, such as vanilla or jasmine.

■ While lying on your sides spooning, take his hand and cup it around your breast, and hug his knees inside the backs of yours. Men aren't wired to be verbal after having an orgasm, but this move will make you two feel connected without even having to speak.

■ He may not be in the mood to talk, but he can definitely listen. Try something mellow, and have the remote to your stereo or iPod near the bed so you can hit "play" without getting up.

■ Many guys love lounging in bed after sex but crave physical space on the mattress. If your man is one of them, create nonsexual intimacy by lying on your backs and holding hands.

■ Leave him in the bed, then

"Is it safe to look now?"

ZZZZZ....
Don't take it personally if he falls asleep after sex. An orgasm activates the parasympathetic nervous system, which controls the "rest and digest" function of the body.

take a warm washcloth and gently towel him off in his below-the-belt region. His body temperature will be up postclimax, but don't use a cool cloth or it will be too jarring—the sensation of the warm heat will feel more pleasurable.

■ If the weather is nice outside, crack open a window, pull just the top sheet over your bodies, and let the fresh air gently cool you off. If you can drift off to sleep, all the better.

■ Or after a few minutes of rest, lead him into the shower. Gently shampooing each other's hair and washing each other's skin—especially with a frothy, fresh-smelling body wash—is sexy in a nurturing way. ■

SOURCES: SEXOLOGIST AVA CADELL, PHD, AUTHOR OF *STOCK MARKET ORGASM*; CERTIFIED SEX EDUCATOR LOU PAGET, AUTHOR OF *THE GREAT LOVER PLAYBOOK*; LINDA R. MONA, PHD, DIRECTOR OF RESEARCH FOR MYPLEASURE.COM

How to Tell If She's Satisfied ...or Not

1 She Gets Up to Do Stuff

When a woman is sexually gratified, she'll usually crave contact via cuddling, talking, or wanting to go for round two, says Darcy Luadzers, PhD, author of *The Ten-Minute Sexual Solution.* "When she's dissatisfied, she'll detach, which could entail rolling over or getting out of bed."

So if she bolts to the kitchen to make a snack, clicks on the television, calls a friend, or starts filing her nails, it's not good, buddy. (Sorry, but you want the cold, hard truth, don't you?) "Busying herself means that those things were either on her mind during the act or she wasn't satisfied and this is how she's channeling her frustration," says Tracey Cox, author of *Superhotsex.*

2 Her Praise Is Too Pat

"'Great' sounds positive, but her one-word summary could mean that she wants more and isn't telling you," says Cox.

But don't get discouraged (easier said than done, we know). Simply break the silence with humor. Then ask what would really make her toes curl. A woman who wasn't turned on the first time can become very sexual when she gets encouragement from her man to ask for more. Fostering an environment where you can both voice your desires—and in some cases, your dissatisfaction—is ultimately one of the best things you can do for your bedroom life.

3 She Is Physically Amped

A much better alternative to asking the question "Did you come?" is to look for the telltale signs yourself.

In the immediate aftermath of a satisfying sack session, her breathing will be rapid, then slowly start to resume to a normal rhythm. Another clue that you rocked her world: Her skin, especially around the neck and chest area, might be flushed.

SAY THIS TO HER RIGHT AFTER SEX

Even if you did successfully show her a good time your job's not done...yet.

"That felt incredible."

WHY SHE NEEDS TO HEAR IT:
Women feel performance anxiety too, so she wants reassurance that's she's skilled in bed. Kudos increases her confidence.

"Your body is so sexy."

WHY SHE NEEDS TO HEAR IT:
Intercourse can cause a woman to feel vulnerable and exposed, so praising her amazing stomach, for example, will boost how she feels when she's naked.

"So, uh, what's your name again?"

WHY SHE NEEDS TO HEAR IT:
Because she wants sex to have some levity and this line lends that...as long as you truly are kidding!

"How are you doing?"

WHY SHE NEEDS TO HEAR IT:
She feels more bonded to you after sex, so checking in with her feeds her need to connect.

It starts with a
little footsie, then
the next thing
you know, you're
at it again!

Revving Up for Round Two

▶ Sometimes winding down leads right into starting up again. And indulging in a second mattress session could increase your orgasmic potential because, according to Joan Elizabeth Lloyd, who writes about sex, when your body is still turned on from a previous round, it's easier to climax. Plus, chances are your man won't come as quickly the second time, so he'll have more time to dedicate to pleasing you.

But you can't just expect sex after sex. And it's certainly not smart to demand it, because when it comes to repeat performances, women have an

anatomical advantage. "As long as she's aroused and lubricated, a woman is physically capable of having sex as many times as she wants without a break in between," explains Drogo K. Montague, MD, of the Cleveland Clinic Glickman Urological Institute.

Guys, however, aren't so lucky. No matter how sexed up their minds are, their members need

While you want to allow for a refractory period, don't give him too much space or there's a good chance he'll doze off.

time to recharge. "On average, a man in his 20s needs 5 to 30 minutes following his first orgasm to attain an erection again," says Dr. Montague. (A 30something dude will need a few more minutes of recovery time; the older the man, the longer it takes for him to get that second erection.) That's because after a guy ejaculates, the muscles in his penis automatically relax, and the blood flow that caused his erection in the first place decreases.

Your strategy: Give him time to recuperate while keeping him sexually focused. To do that, tell him how good he makes you feel—a carnal compliment strokes his ego and keeps his brain tuned to sex. One detail worth noting: Stick to the present tense. Avoid saying such things as "That was great, big guy, but I'm still raring to go and time's a wastin'." Telling him how hot he was signals that it's over. Instead, say how hot he is and you'll subliminally help him segue into round two.

But while you want to allow a refractory period, don't give him too much space or there's a chance he'll doze off—or worse, turn on the TV! That said, you also can't pounce on his penis like it's the last cute skirt on the sale rack. "After a guy ejaculates, his penis is ultrasensitive," says Lloyd. "If

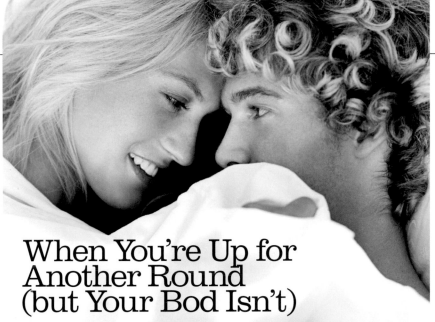

When You're Up for Another Round (but Your Bod Isn't)

If your south-of-the-border region is a little spent postsex, try:

Lubing Up

It's normal not to feel lubricated enough for a second time, so don't worry that something is wrong with your sex drive. A water-based lubricant will do the trick. Just a few dabs can prevent soreness and help get your natural juices flowing again.

Hitting the Shower

Sometimes you feel too icky-sticky after sex for a second session. Slip away for a between-rounds shower (with or without your guy). You'll feel clean, refreshed, and lickable again, and your body will be revitalized.

Calling It a Night

If your vaginal area is sore, swollen, or stings after the first round, then quit. Besides being painful, tiny abrasions may leave you more susceptible to infection, even when you're using condoms. Sex isn't an endurance contest, so be smart enough to say "when."

you touch him there even gently following a climax, he'll probably yelp." A good plan of action is to try some innocent yet arousing body contact. "After he's caught his breath, curl up against him so your tush grazes his crotch," suggests Lloyd. "Or if he's on his belly, arch your body on top of him and let just your nipples skim his back."

Then start caressing his chest, back, and shoulders. The point is to be suggestive and playful, not demanding. "If he thinks that you're giving him an ultimatum about having sex again, he might worry so much about getting it up that it won't happen at all," says Lloyd. After several minutes, your man should be ready for a more direct hands-on approach. Start his engine by brushing your lips against his testicles, then move on to his shaft. "Just work up to touching or licking the head of his penis slowly—it stays sensitive the longest after orgasm," says Lloyd.

While men in their 20s and early 30s should have no problem getting it up twice in a night, you need to remember that there are different degrees of penis rigidity—just because he's not wielding a rock-hard erection the entire time doesn't mean he's not into having sex with you.

Instead, enjoy all phases of his longer-if-not-stronger erection, and feel free to take intercourse breaks to allow for other action. You may decide to stop and just kiss—hard and deep—while his penis rebounds. Or you may ask for a little manual magic while reminding him of how great he's making you feel.

SECOND-TIME SUGGESTIONS

Whether you haven't had your big O yet—or you just want more, you greedy girl!—you can use this repeat performance to sample some new positions, act out fantasies, or alter the tone and tempo of the encounter. And the second time around

Fun game: Let the dice decide how many kisses or licks you lavish on each other at a time.

"Concentrate on teasing each other, talking dirty, or any other seductive moves that require a little imagination."

doesn't have to be just a rerun— a slower, deeper, and more intense experience can come after a wham-bam session. "The follow-up round is usually less frantic, so you have more time to indulge secret desires and dream up sexy scenarios," says Lloyd.

"Without that erotic urgency, you can concentrate on teasing each other with foreplay, talking dirty, role-playing, and other seductive moves that take a little time and imagination."

There's a practical reason to change things up too—if your

man did most of the work initially, it's only fair for you to take the power position next.

Think of your night of recurring delight as if it were a road trip—he drives for the first leg, then you take the wheel in the home stretch and allow him to kick back. That might mean you on top this time, a move designed for your pleasure since you get to control the pace and pressure. Or you can try spoon-style sex, where you lie with his chest to your back.

You don't always have to make a major modification to your erotic repertoire to snag sequel benefits. Small mood changes such as putting in a new CD, lighting a few candles, or leading each other to a different room in the house will get you both so cranked up, you may even want to go for round three.

MORE ECSTASY EXTENDERS

■ Give him a reverse strip-tease. Let him watch you dress up in a lacy bra and panties or a sexy, skimpy dress with nothing on underneath.

■ Brush different parts of your body—your fingertips, the ends of your hair, your cheeks, your breasts—past his lips. There are big concentrations of nerve endings on the lips, which are extremely sensitive to touch and will quickly raise his arousal levels.

■ Have a heavy make-out session, alternating long, open-mouthed kisses with gentle nibbling. Kissing makes pleasure endorphins skyrocket.

■ Create anticipation by suggesting a spicy new twist. The perfect example: "The next time we have sex, I'd like to try doing it in front of a full-length mir-

This will get his blood sugar back up!

your grasp, "stir" them in circles, until you're gently spreading his cheeks.

And guess what? By doing so, you're also indirectly stimulating his package from an exciting new angle—which is an unexpectedly intense way to get his blood flow-

Feed each other sensual foods—ideally, bite-size snacks that contain fat and sugar, such as chocolate.

ror." Boom! You've planted a visual that he will be eager to bring to life as soon as he is physically able to do so.

■ Switch up your usual back massage routine and treat him to a gluteus-maximus rubdown: Turn him on his stomach and start by gently kneading his buns, then with some flesh in

ing down there for round two.

■ Feed each other sensual foods to get your blood sugar back up, among other things. Bite-size snacks that have some fat and sugar, such as chocolate and ice cream, will do the trick. ■

SOURCES: SEXOLOGIST AVA CADELL, PHD, AUTHOR OF *STOCK MARKET ORGASM*; CERTIFIED SEX EDUCATOR LOU PAGET, AUTHOR OF *THE GREAT LOVER PLAYBOOK*; LINDA R. MONA, PHD, DIRECTOR OF RESEARCH FOR MYPLEASURE.COM

Clean up, so you can get dirty again.

What He Thinks About Postsex

Listen in as guys confess the thoughts that run through their minds after doing the deed.

"I'm so spent after sex, my brain is in this happy, half-functioning mode. I'm not capable of intelligent speech—all I want to do is enjoy the moment." —Charles

"After sex, my body is one giant pleasure receptor. Food—whether it's a big bowl of cereal or last night's Chinese takeout leftovers—seems to taste so much better." —Dan

"It's not that I don't like spooning after sex. But when I've spent half an hour supporting all of my weight on one elbow or working up a decent sweat, I really want to stretch out." —Wayne

"When my fiancée and I have amazing sex, I think to myself, Man, I hope we're still screwing like that in 20 years." —Ted

"I like to switch to a totally different subject. I usually think about sports. I contemplate what players I should add to my fantasy baseball league." —Andrew

"I love to cuddle afterward. The feeling of my girlfriend's skin against mine, the blankets keeping us warm, the togetherness... I'm in a state of pure satisfaction." —Ian

"After sex, give me cartoons or Pink Floyd. I love watching something that's not real or listening to something spacey. It brings me around slowly and softly." —Pablo

"I replay the highlights in my mind—the foreplay moves that made my girlfriend moan, any hot stuff she said or noises she made, and of course, the look on her face when she had an orgasm." —Doug

"My penis shrivels once I climax, so I'm thinking, damn, I hope she doesn't notice as I reach for my boxers. Any guy who tells you he doesn't stress about shrinkage is lying...or huge." —Rex

"This is gonna sound sleazy, but I run my numbers. If a girl was a great lay, I add her to my tally." —Jerry

"When I first meet a woman, I imagine what she'll be like in the sack. If she's a freak on the dance floor, she'll probably be a freak in bed too. Then afterward, I assess whether she lived up to my expectations." —Mylos

"After doing it, I like to get out of bed and get a drink or have a shower right away. It's not the closeness that I mind, but I find it boring to just lie there doing nothing when my mind is activated." —Bill

"Sure, sex makes me feel a little tired, but I never feel weak. In fact, I feel the exact opposite, like I can take on the whole world." —Chris

Indulging in erotic reading has numerous benefits. For starters, it's incredibly titillating, so it's a great way to get yourself in the mood for sex. Not only that, but the characters' risqué behavior can provide you with new ideas for your own bedroom escapades. This collection of steamy stories—all Cosmo originals—are sure to inspire plenty of lust. Why not read them aloud to your lover tonight?

When she got close to his tan skin she
could tell there was a manly, musky scent to it.

A Frisky Foreign Affair

Jules hadn't taken a vacation in two years. Though she loved being a lawyer, she desperately needed to get away. So she booked a weeklong trip to the Caribbean. During the day, she relaxed in the sun and swam in the ocean. Nights were reserved for hanging out at the hotel bar with the sexy bartender, Daniel.

Jules was drawn to more than just Daniel's tight body. Their lives were polar opposites, and she found his carefree spirit contagious. They chatted about everything under the sun. Jules had a weakness for sexy accents, and Daniel's was no exception—in fact, it made her weak in the knees.

They had made plans for Daniel to show her a secluded beach on the last day of her vacation. She pulled on a skimpy bikini and a sarong.

As she waited in the lobby of the hotel, she caught sight of him walking toward her. His linen shirt was unbuttoned, revealing his taut chest.

"Shall we?" he asked with a smile, holding out his arm for her to take.

After a walk through a wooded area, they neared the beach. Jules paused to appreciate the beauty of the crystal-clear water crashing onto the shore. Suddenly, Daniel whispered in her ear, "It's almost as beautiful as you are." She smiled demurely and ran her fingers through her hair.

"You have incredible hands," he said, watching her intently. "So delicate." Turning to him, Jules smiled. "Hmm, someone's itchin' for a massage," she teased. "Well, if you're offering," he said, turning his back to her.

Jules caressed his neck. Then she reached up under his shirt and rubbed his broad shoulders before turning him around.

"You feel incredible," she murmured, leaning into his warm body. There was a musky scent to his tan, muscular skin.

As she was enjoying lavishing his bronze torso with attention, he grabbed her hand and led her to a dune where they were hidden from view. His hands gently grazed her arms, back, and shoulders and traveled down her sides

over and over again. When she couldn't hold out any longer, she lifted Daniel's head and slid her body down until he was positioned directly over her. After slipping on a condom, he pressed all of himself into Jules,

His hands traveled down to her bikini bottom. He tucked his fingers teasingly inside.

until they met her bikini bottom. He tucked his fingers teasingly inside and traced a trail across her pelvis and around to her butt. She shuddered with desire.

Using her sarong to shield her skin from the sand, Daniel lay Jules down and inched off her bikini as she stripped off his shorts. Then he drew his tongue down her stomach and below until he hit her hottest spot

sending her into a state of otherworldly pleasure.

As they moved in a perfect in-and-out tempo, Daniel gazed into Jules's eyes—as if they'd been lovers for a long time. His face glistened with sweat. He smiled and kissed her deeply. Jules took in every gorgeous feature on his face, then closed her eyes and wished she could take him home as a souvenir.

Dial "M" for Moan

The telephone repairman was early and obviously impatient. Before Jocelyn could answer the door, he buzzed again. She was ready to scold him until she opened the door...and her jaw dropped. Tall and handsome, he was dressed in jeans and a tee shirt that barely contained his chiseled chest. His dark hair fell to his high cheekbones. "Sorry I didn't answer on the first ring," Jocelyn apologized. "That's okay," he said. "The telephone man always rings twice."

She smiled. "That's the postman."

"Oh, yeah," he said with a grin.

She let him in and explained the problem. After fooling with the jack for a few minutes, he said it had to be rewired due to a torn cable. "This is going to take a while."

Jocelyn's pulse raced. "Fine by me."

"Nice place," he said. "All yours?"

"Yeah, first time without a roommate."

"First times are exciting," he said, looking directly into her eyes.

His innuendo surprised her. "Uh, yeah. Would you care for a drink?" she stammered. "A beer?"

"No, thank you. I'm supposed to be on my best behavior on the job, though I guess exceptions can be made."

"Like what?" she asked, hoping he'd make a move. He strode over to her and, without any hesitation, kissed her.

He looked at her for the go-ahead. She whimpered, and he pulled her on top of him, sliding her skirt up to her waist.

They'd barely exchanged words, and Jocelyn was afraid to move, fearing she'd break the spell. He sensed her hesitation. "Just lie back," he said. As he pulled off his shirt, her palms seemed to melt on his skin. Cupping her hands, he led them to his jeans and asked "Can you feel how much I want you?"

Unable to speak, she nodded. He stripped off his pants and rolled on the condom he just happened to be carrying with him. Jocelyn eyed every luscious inch of him. Dropping to his knees, he leaned over her body. She lifted her hips and wrapped her legs around his back. She felt as though she was being consumed under the weight of his body. Her limbs tingled, and she let herself go completely. Utterly satisfied, she lay there, and he fell beside her. When they caught their breath, Jocelyn turned to him and smiled. "Now, about the telephone man always ringing twice...."

Cupping her hands, he led them to his jeans and said, "Can you feel how much I want you?"

Making the Big Score

Anita never missed class and rarely drank. But with graduation a month away, she was tired of doing the right thing. And Ian—a strapping rugby player—spoke directly to her erotic alter ego. She had admired him for four years, and she couldn't ignore her desires any longer.

Ian was sitting on the sidelines watching the season's last rugby game. Even with a cast on his leg, he looked sexy. He'd injured himself a few weeks earlier, and Anita ached to nurse him back to health. She made her way over.

"Excuse me, Ian?" she asked.

He turned to her and smiled. His hazel eyes flickered with specks of gold, and the fine scar on his cheek made him look even more masculine.

"I'm Anita. I work in the phys-ed department. Assistant coach Brown wants to see you in the locker room."

"I'm gonna need help getting down those stairs," he said, eyeing his cast.

Everything was going as she had planned. "Don't worry. I'll lend you a hand," she said, trying to sound casual.

She put one hand on his arm and one on his shoulder. As he hobbled down the stairs, her heart pounded in her chest as she prayed that her seduction scheme would be successful.

Ian, set his crutches aside, and took his large hands in hers, leading him to the nearest bench. She traced the curve of his jaw with her pinkie nail. She hungrily kissed his neck and slid her tongue down to his collarbone. He reached to unbutton her shirt, but she entwined her fingers with his. "Uh-uh, me first," she said.

With Ian pinned beneath her, Anita could do what she pleased to his brawny body. She pulled off his jersey and began kissing his broad chest and six-pack abs. Drawing herself back to his lips, Anita aggressively plunged her tongue deep into his mouth.

Ian's moans unleashed the bad girl she always knew was inside. She slid off her skirt and inched up his torso, kneeling over him until his mouth was

When they stepped inside the empty locker room, he looked around and asked, "Where's Coach Brown?"

"Well," Anita said, biting her lip, "I have a confession to make. The coach didn't want to see you. I did."

"Ooookay," he said, looking confused. "I have wanted you ever since I first laid eyes on you," she whispered.

"I have a confession too," he said. "I've seen you around and wondered why it was taking you so long to talk to me."

That was all she needed. Anita made her way over to

229

beneath her. Lowering herself, she let him tease her into a frenzy. Needing to feel him inside her, she unzipped his pants and climbed on top of him. They found a wild, unbridled rhythm. "God, you're incredible!" Ian muttered, as they moved in tandem. Her body tightened before reaching a glorious release. Anita lifted herself off his glistening body to catch her breath as Ian gently wiped beads of sweat from her breastbone. For Anita, it felt almost as good as wiping away her good-girl reputation.

Risqué Business With the Boss

Ken was Stacey's dream boss. He gave her insight, support, and 9-to-5 eye candy. Though nearing 50, Ken was the ultimate sexy older man with a fit physique and eyes that exuded confidence.

Ken and Stacey did everything they could to ignore the sexual tension that simmered between them, but late-night deadlines didn't help. Stacey's willpower had been put to the test for the past grueling week. She prayed she wouldn't succumb to her desires when they were alone in that secluded conference room.

As they put the finishing touches on a big proposal, one teeny brush from Ken sent Stacey's libido into overdrive. "You've done it again, Stacey," Ken complimented her, grazing her arm with the flat of his hand. "This is your best work." Just having his broad fingers caressing her made Stacey tingle.

A deep yearning triggered inside her. And the feeling seemed to be mutual.

"Stacey, I hope I'm not being out of line here," Ken whispered. "But how are you still single?"

She smiled. "Guess I'm just waiting for the right man."

"Ahh, if only I could peel off 25 years," he lamented.

She knew she was crossing into forbidden territory when she said, "I'd say you're fine. More than fine."

He smiled as she grabbed the files. But the folders slipped from her grip and fell to the floor.

"Ugh, it's spreadsheet hell," she said with a laugh. She kneeled down to pick up the files, and he gave her a hand. Their eyes locked, and hesitantly, Ken moved in closer to her. After months of stifling her deepest cravings, she couldn't resist. Surrendering to her lust, she backed him up against the row of filing cabinets. He responded by kissing Stacey's face. Then he unbuttoned her blazer.

"God, Stacey, I've dreamed of doing this for so long," he murmured, as his hands eagerly slipped under her silky bra.

She trembled under his expert touch. Soon, her skirt and panties were on the floor as she clawed at his shirt and suit trousers. Naked, she reveled in the heat of his sturdy body. He devoured her with his eyes. "You take my breath away," he said. Their lips met, and her tongue hungrily explored his mouth. She succumbed to the pleasure that had threatened to bubble over for so long, like champagne in a fluted glass.

Propping her on the conference table, Ken touched her as only an experienced man could, running his hands down her tummy and over her legs. He seemed to know instinctively just where to go and how long to stay. Using his strong arms, Ken lifted her hips to him. He felt incredible, and she begged him not to stop. He gladly obliged, slowly bringing her to the peak of ecstasy.

As the excitement of consummating their libidinous urges buzzed through them, they kissed softly, falling into each other's arms. Looking at their clothes strewn across the conference-room floor, they laughed, promising to end all of their torturously long meetings in this very memorable way. ∎

ABOUT OUR EXPERTS

RACHEL CARLTON ABRAMS, MD, founder of Redwood Circle, a medical center for the healing arts in Capitola, California, and coauthor of *The Multi-Orgasmic Woman: How Any Woman Can Experience Ultimate Pleasure and Dramatically Enhance Her Health and Happiness*

SADIE ALLISON, DHS, sex educator and author of *Tickle His Pickle: Your Hands-On Guide to Penis Pleasing*, *Tickle Your Fancy: A Woman's Guide to Sexual Self-Pleasure*, and *Toygasms!: The Insider's Guide to Sex Toys and Techniques*

MARGOT ANAND, producer of the DVD trilogy *Margot Anand's Secret Keys to the Ultimate Love Life* and author of *The New Art of Sexual Ecstasy*

MICHAEL BADER, DMH, psychologist, psychoanalyst, and author of *Arousal: The Secret Logic of Sexual Fantasies*

JAMES BARADA, MD, director of the Albany Center for Sexual Health

LONNIE BARBACH, PHD, clinical faculty at the University of California San Francisco School of Medicine and author of *For Each Other: Sharing Sexual Intimacy* and *For Yourself: The Fulfillment of Female Sexuality*

LAURA BERMAN, PHD, assistant clinical professor of ob-gyn/psychiatry at the Feinberg School of Medicine at Northwestern University, director of the Berman Center in Chicago, and author of *The Passion Prescription: Ten Weeks to Your Best Sex—Ever!*

ROBERT W. BIRCH, PHD, Ohio certified sexologist

LADAWN BLACK, author of *Let's Get It On: 15 Hot Tips and Tricks to Spice Up Your Sex Life* and *Stripped Bare: The 12 Truths That Will Help You Land the Very Best Black Man*

JOEL D. BLOCK, PHD, psychologist, sex therapist, and author of *The Art of the Quickie: Fast Sex, Fast Orgasm, Anytime, Anywhere*

ROCHELLE BLOOM, president of the Fragrance Foundation

STEVE BODANKSY, PHD, coauthor of *To Bed or Not to Bed: What Men Want, What Women Want, How Great Sex Happens*

VERA BODANSKY, PHD, coauthor of *The Illustrated Guide to Extended Massive Orgasm*

VIRGINIA BONOFIGLIO, adjunct professor at the Fashion Institute of Technology in New York City

GLORIA G. BRAME, PHD, clinical sex therapist based in Athens, Georgia, and author of *Come Hither: A Commonsense Guide to Kinky Sex*. Website: gloriabrame.com

PATTI BRITTON, PHD, Los Angeles sex coach, president of the American Association of Sexuality Educators, Counselors, and Therapists, and author of *The Complete Idiot's Guide to Sensual Massage*

MICHAEL BRODER, PHD, Philadelphia psychologist and author of *Can Your Relationship Be Saved?: How to Know Whether to Stay or Go*

AVA CADELL, PHD, founder of online Loveology University and author of *The Pocket Idiot's Guide to Oral Sex* and *Stock Market Orgasm: Secrets to Expanding Your Sexual Portfolio*

WILLIAM CANE, author of *The Art of Kissing*

GILDA CARLE, PHD, relationship expert in New York, professor of psychology and communications at Mercy College, in Dobbs Ferry, New York, and author of *Don't Bet on the Prince!: How to Have the Man You Want By Betting on Yourself*

TRACEY COX, sex and relationship expert and author of *Superhotsex*

MITCHELL CREININ, MD, director of family planning, and professor of obstetrics, gynecology, and reproductive sciences at the University of Pittsburgh School of Medicine

JOY DAVIDSON, PHD, New York City sex therapist, producer of the online video series *The Joy Spot*, and author of *Fearless Sex: A Babe's Guide to Overcoming Your Romantic Obsessions and Getting the Sex Life You Deserve*

GAYLE DELANEY, PHD, founding president of the International Association for the Study of Dreams, codirector of the Delaney and Flowers Dream Center in San Francisco, and author of *All About Dreams: Everything You Need to Know About Why We Have Them, What They Mean, and How to Put Them to Work for You*

HOWARD DEVORE, PHD, San Francisco psychologist and sex therapist

FELICE DUNAS, PHD, Los Angeles relationship coach and author of *Passion Play: Ancient Secrets for a Lifetime of Health and Happiness Through Sensational Sex*

RICHARD EBSTEIN, PHD, director of the Scheinfeld Center for Human Genetics in the Social Sciences at the Hebrew University of Jerusalem

DONALD ETKES, PHD, Los Angeles sex therapist and author of *Loving With Passion: Your Guide to the Joy of Sexual Intimacy* (available on sexesteem.com)

PATRICIA FARRELL, PHD, licensed psychologist and author of *How to Be Your Own Therapist: A Step-by-Step Guide to Taking Back Your Life*

HELEN FISHER, PHD, anthropologist and author of *Why We Love: The Nature and Chemistry of Romantic Love*

WILLIAM FITZGERALD, PHD, retired sex therapist in San Jose, California, and guest lecturer at San Jose State University

MEGAN FLEMING, PHD, New York City clinical psychologist and certified sex therapist, assistant clinical professor of psychiatry at Albert Einstein College of Medicine of Yeshiva University, and founder and former director of the Sexual Health Rehabilitation Program at Beth Israel Medical Center

MELINDA GALLAGHER, founder of CAKE, an entertainment and educational company promoting female sexual empowerment and coauthor of *The Hot Woman's Handbook: The CAKE Guide to Female Sexual Pleasure*

SANDOR GARDOS, PHD, sex therapist and founder of MyPleasure.com

PATRICIA GARFIELD, PHD, cofounder and former president of the International Association for the Study of Dreams and author of *The Universal Dream Key: The 12 Most Common Dream Themes Around the World*

ADAM GLICKMAN, CEO of Condomania.com

MARC GOLDSTEIN, MD, professor of reproductive medicine and urology and surgeon-in-chief of male reproductive medicine and surgery at New York–Presbyterian Hospital/Weill Cornell Medical Center in New York City

JACQUIE NOELLE GREAUX, coauthor of *Better Sex Through Yoga: Easy Routines to Boost Your Sex Drive, Enhance Physical Pleasure, and Spice Up Your Bedroom Life*

GILLIAN HOLLOWAY, PHD, dream-analysis expert and author of *Erotic Dreams: The Secret to Understanding Women's Hidden Passions*

HILDA HUTCHERSON, MD, clinical professor of obstetrics and gynecology at Columbia University Medical Center and author of *What Your Mother Never Told You About Sex*

BARBARA KEESLING, PHD, lecturer in human sexuality at California State University at Fullerton, and author of *The Good Girl's Guide to Bad Girl Sex*

IAN KERNER, PHD, New York sex therapist and author of *She Comes First: The Thinking Man's Guide to Pleasuring a Woman* and *He Comes Next: The Thinking Woman's Guide to Pleasuring a Man*

KATE KOBAK, a New York certified instructor in the Alexander Technique

JUDY KURIANSKY, PHD, New York sex therapist, instructor at Columbia University Teachers College, and author of *The Complete Idiot's Guide to Tantric Sex*

DEB LEVINE, executive director of Internet Sexuality Information Services in Oakland, California, adjunct professor in human sexuality at San Francisco State University, and author of *The Joy of Cybersex: A Guide for Creative Lovers*

LAURENCE LEVINE, MD, professor of urology and director of the Male Sexual Function and Fertility Program at Rush University Medical Center in Chicago and president of the Sexual Medicine Society of North America

LOGAN LEVKOFF, sexologist and sexuality educator and author of *Third Base Ain't What It Used to Be: What Your Kids Are Learning About Sex—and What They Can Still Learn to Be Sexually Healthy Adults*

JOAN ELIZABETH LLOYD, author of *The Perfect Orgasm: How to Get It, How to Give It* and *Hot Summer Nights* (fiction)

DARCY LUADZERS, PHD, certified sex therapist and author of *The Ten-Minute Sexual Solution: A Busy Couple's Guide to Having More Fun, Intimacy, and Sex*

ABOUT OUR EXPERTS

BAT SHEVA MARCUS, clinical director of the Medical Center for Female Sexuality in Purchase, New York

I. DAVID MARCUS, PHD, psychologist at Silicon Valley Psychotherapy Center in San Jose, California

SHELDON MARKS, MD, assistant clinical professor of urology at the University of Arizona College of Medicine, director of the International Center for Vasectomy Reversal, and WebMD.com men's health expert

JEANNE MARRAZZO, MD, associate professor of infectious diseases at the University of Washington

LISA MASTERSON, MD, ob-gyn at Cedars-Sinai Medical Center in Los Angeles and founder of Ocean Oasis Medical Day Spa in Santa Monica, California

LESLIE MILLER, MD, clinical associate professor of obstetrics and gynecology at the University of Washington, in Seattle

LINDA R. MONA, PHD, licensed clinical psychologist and director of research for MyPleasure.com

DROGO K. MONTAGUE, MD, section head of prosthetic surgery and genitourethral reconstruction at the Cleveland Clinic Glickman Urological Institute

CARO NESS, author of *Secrets of Dreams*

LOU PAGET, certified sex educator and author of *The Great Lover Playbook: 365 Tips and Techniques to Keep the Fires Burning All Year Long* and *Orgasms: How to Have Them, Give Them, and Keep Them Coming*

CAROL QUEEN, PHD, staff sexologist at goodvibes .com

HOWARD J. RUPPEL JR., PHD, chancellor of the Institute for Advanced Study of Human Sexuality

MARK SCHWARTZ, SCD, clinical codirector of Castlewood Treatment Center in Saint Louis and adjunct associate professor in the departments of psychiatry and obstetrics and gynecology at Saint Louis University School of Medicine

JUDITH SEIFER, PHD, sex therapist, professor of sexual health at the Institute for Advanced Study of Human Sexuality in San Francisco, and past president of the American Association of Sexuality Educators, Counselors, and Therapists

MICHAEL SEILER, PHD, Chicago marital-sex therapist

KENNETH RAY STUBBS, PHD, certified sexologist and author of *Kiss of Desire: A Guide to Oral Sex for Men and Women*

TROY SURRAT, global consulting makeup artist for Maybelline New York

PATRICIA TAYLOR, PHD, author of *Expanded Orgasm: Soar to Ecstasy at Your Lover's Every Touch*

BONNIE EAKER WEIL, PHD, New York City relationship therapist and author of *Make Up, Don't Break Up: Finding and Keeping Love for Singles and Couples*

DAVID WEISS, PHD, board-certified sex therapist, clinical psychologist, and ob-gyn consulting staff at UMass Memorial Medical Center in Worcester, Massachusetts

LOUANNE COLE WESTON, PHD, sex therapist in Fair Oaks, California, and author of WebMD.com "Sex Matters" blog

BEVERLY WHIPPLE, PHD, secretary general of the World Association for Sexual Health and coauthor of *The G-Spot and Other Discoveries About Human Sexuality* and *The Science of Orgasm*

ALINE P. ZOLDBROD, PHD, Boston sex therapist and coauthor of *Sex Talk: Uncensored Exercises for Exploring What Really Turns You On*

PHOTO CREDITS

Cover

Robert Delahanty

Table of Contents

PAGE 5: Jack Miskell; Rodolfo Martinez
PAGE 6-7: Wadley; Svend Lindbaek; Jack Miskell

Preplay

PAGE 12-13: Tamara Schlesinger
PAGE 14-15: Svend Lindbaek; Tamara Schlesinger
PAGE 16-17: Tamara Schlesinger (2)
PAGE 18-19: Robert Delahanty
PAGE 20-21: Anna Palma; istockphoto.com
PAGE 22: Beth Studenberg
PAGE 24-25: Asha Fuller
PAGE 26: Asha Fuller
PAGE 28: Jack Miskell
PAGE 30-31: Jack Miskell; Asha Fuller
PAGE 32-33: Noel J. Federizo; Mark Leibowitz; Jack Miskell
PAGE 34-39: Rodolfo Martinez
PAGE 40-41: Eric McNatt
PAGE 42-43: Jeffrey Westbrook/Studio D (2); Tamara Schlesinger; Gabe Palmer/Alamy
PAGE 44-45: Tamara Schlesinger; Jeffrey Westbrook/ Studio D
PAGE 46-47: Asha Fuller; Noel J. Federizo
PAGE 48-49: Noel J. Federizo
PAGE 50-51: Creatas/fotosearch.com; Tamara Schlesinger
PAGE 52-53: Jack Miskell; (frame) Corbis/punchstock. com; (male model) Joe Schmelzer; Robert Delahanty
PAGE 54-55: fotosearch.com; Drew and Derek Riker; Ruy Sanchez Blanco

Foreplay

PAGE 58-59: Tamara Schlesinger
PAGE 61: Eric McNatt
PAGE 62: Svend Lindbaek
PAGE 64-65: Rodolfo Martinez
PAGE 66: Rodolfo Martinez
PAGE 68-69: Cristina Tarantola
PAGE 70-71: Roger Cabello; Svend Lindbaek

PAGE 72-73: Cristina Tarantola
PAGE 74-75: Tamara Schlesinger (4)
PAGE 76-77: Jeffrey Westbrook/Studio D.; David Cook; Svend Lindbaek
PAGE 78-79: Beth Studenberg (2)
PAGE 80: David Turner/Studio D
PAGE 82: Asha Fuller
PAGE 84-85: Tamara Schlesinger (2)
PAGE 86-87: Svend Lindbaek
PAGE 88-89: Hemera Technologies/Alamy; Svend Lindbaek
PAGE 90-91: Beth Studenberg
PAGE 92-93: Ruy Sanchez Blanco
PAGE 95: Wadley
PAGE 96-97: Chris Eckert/Studio D
PAGE 99: Ruy Sanchez Blanco
PAGE 101: Alex Cao
PAGE 102-103: Tamara Schlesinger
PAGE 104-105: Mark Lund; Davies + Starr; Mary Evan Picture Library/Alamy; David Cook; Davies + Starr
PAGE 106-107: Eric Cahan; Anna Palma
PAGE 108-109: Tamara Schlesinger
PAGE 110: Tamara Schlesinger
PAGE 112-113: David Turner/Studio D; Tamara Schlesinger
PAGE 114-115: Jack Miskell
PAGE 117: Tamara Schlesinger; Jack Miskell
PAGE 118-119: Jack Miskell (2)

Main Event

PAGE 122-123: Wadley
PAGE 124-125: Jack Miskell; Tamara Schlesinger
PAGE 126: Tamara Schlesinger
PAGE 128: Jack Miskell
PAGE 131: Anna Palma
PAGE 132-133: Asha Fuller
PAGE 134-157: (Illustrations) John Pirman
PAGE 156: Wadley
PAGE 158-159: Lush Pix/fotosearch.com
PAGE 160-161: Tamara Schlesinger; Davies + Starr
PAGE 162-163: fotosearch.com; Tamara Schlesinger; Svend Lindbaek
PAGE 164-165: Eric McNatt; Chris Fanning
PAGE 166-167: Tamara Schlesinger

PAGE 168: Asha Fuller
PAGE 170-171: Tamara Schlesinger
PAGE 172-173: Rita Maas/Envision; fotosearch.com; Tamara Schlesinger
PAGE 174-175: Tamara Schlesinger; (camera) usa.canon.com; (couple) Tamara Schlesinger; Photographer's Choice/Getty Images
PAGE 176-177: David Cook; Tamara Schlesinger; fotosearch.com; Steve Wisbauer/stuff
PAGE 178-179: Anne Fougedoire Ferrez
PAGE 181: Jack Miskell
PAGE 182-183: Wadley
PAGE 185: Wadley
PAGE 186-187: Mark Leibowitz; Anna Palma
PAGE 188-189: Ruy Sanchez Blanco
PAGE 190: Tamara Schlesinger
PAGE 192-193: Wadley
PAGE 194-195: Asha Fuller
PAGE 196-197: Svend Lindbaek; Chris Fanning
PAGE 198-199: Michael Prince/Corbis; Anna Palma
PAGE 200: Jack Miskell; Beth Studenberg
PAGE 202-203: Jeffrey Westbrook/Studio D; Asha Fuller

Afterplay

PAGE 206-207: Beth Studenberg
PAGE 208-209: Tamara Schlesinger
PAGE 210-211: Eric McNatt
PAGE 212-213: Beth Studenberg
PAGE 214-215: Jack Miskell; Tamara Schlesinger
PAGE 216-217: Ruy Sanchez Blanco; Alex Cao
PAGE 218-219: Jack Miskell; Cristina Tarantola
PAGE 220-221: Butch Hogan; Eric McNatt

Red-Hot Reads

PAGE 224-225: Beth Studenberg
PAGE 226-227: Roger Cabello; Tamara Schlesinger
PAGE 228-229: Tamara Schlesinger
PAGE 230-231: Alex Cao; Tamara Schlesinger

The models photographed in *Cosmo's Guide to Red-Hot Sex* are used for illustrative purposes only; *Cosmo's Guide to Red-Hot Sex* does not suggest that the models actually engage in the conduct discussed in the stories they illustrate.

INDEX

INDEX

COSMOPOLITAN

TEXT BY Michele Promaulayko
EDITED BY John Searles
BOOK DESIGN BY Peter Perron
POSITION ILLUSTRATIONS BY John Pirman
ASSISTANT EDITOR Victoria Lucia

EDITOR-IN-CHIEF Kate White
DESIGN DIRECTOR Ann P. Kwong

Library of Congress Cataloging-in-Publication Data

Cosmo's red-hot sex / the editors of Cosmopolitan.
      p. cm.
Includes bibliographical references and index.
1. Sex instruction. 2. Sex. 3. Sexual excitement. I. Cosmopolitan (New York, N.Y. :1952)
HQ31.C8274 2007
613.9'6--dc22   2007010538

10 9 8 7 6 5 4 3 2

First Paperback Edition 2011
Published by Hearst Books
A Division of Sterling Publishing Co., Inc.
387 Park Avenue South, New York, NY 10016

Cosmopolitan is a trademark of Hearst Communications, Inc.

www.cosmopolitan.com

For information about custom editions, special sales, premium and corporate purchases, please contact
Sterling Special Sales Department at 800-805-5489 or specialsales@sterlingpublishing.com.

Distributed in Canada by Sterling Publishing
c/o Canadian Manda Group, 165 Dufferin Street
Toronto, Ontario, Canada M6K 3H6

Distributed in Australia by Capricorn Link (Australia) Pty. Ltd.
P.O. Box 704, Windsor, NSW 2756 Australia

Manufactured in China

Sterling ISBN 978-1-58816-878-8